VILLAGE
CHRISTMASES

With love to my great-granddaughter, Naomi, born July
1991, whose Christmases will be very different to anything
that I have written or experienced.

VILLAGE
CHRISTMASES

MOLLIE HARRIS

ALAN SUTTON

First published in the United Kingdom in 1992
Alan Sutton Publishing Ltd · Far Thrupp · Stroud
Gloucestershire

First published in the United States of America in 1992
Alan Sutton Publishing Inc · Wolfeboro Falls · NH 03896–0848

British Library Cataloguing in Publication Data

Harris, Mollie
Village Christmases
I. Title
394.268282092
ISBN 0-7509-0232-9

Library of Congress Cataloging in Publication Data applied for

Jacket photograph courtesy of Helen Peacocke.
Colour section: Christmas 1991: i Mollie Harris; ii–vii Helen Peacocke;
viii Mr Neelan.

Line illustrations by Martin Latham.

Typeset in Bembo 11/16pt.
Typesetting and origination by
Alan Sutton Publishing Limited.
Colour separation by Yeo Graphics Reproductions Ltd.
Printed in Great Britain by
The Bath Press, Bath, Avon.

Contents

VILLAGE CHRISTMASES

VILLAGE CHRISTMASES

Introduction

I have called my book *Village Christmases* because that's what it is all about – beginning with the Christmases of my extreme youth – some spent at home in Ducklington, others at Sherborne in the Cotswolds, either with my gran and gramp or my uncle and aunt and cousins – and then later on in the village where I now live, Eynsham.

There is absolutely no comparison between the Christmases of today and those of yesteryear – or indeed with everyday life.

So in my book I have tried to convey the expectations and happiness of those far off hard-up Christmas-times. At the same time I have also written about some of my memories of Christmases during the past sixty-odd years, bringing the reader to the present time. But mostly it is about my young days, those unforgettable happy days in the twenties, when almost everybody was in the same boat as us – 'blumen hard-up'! And yet our parents managed to create the surprise, jollity and excitement of Christmas-time.

Mind you, there were no Christmas trees at home, they were unheard of as far as we ordinary folk were concerned –

The church of St Bartholomew, Ducklington

but the wondrous giant tree which came from Cokethorpe Park, the home of Major Guy Feilden and his wife, the Hon. Mrs Feilden is something that I, and the other children that I went to school with at that time, will never forget. There was a gift for everybody on the tree. This was their gift to Ducklington schoolchildren, along with a scrumptious tea, with its wafer-thin bread and butter. Such a contrast to the usual 'door-steps', great thick slices which

Ducklington school. Mollie is probably on the right, second row, with head turned

our mother hacked off, holding the loaf close to her ample
bosom, cursing because we never had a sharp knife; we certainly didn't have such a thing as a bread-board – well, not
in the early days anyhow. And cake at home was a bit of a
luxury: with nine mouths to feed one ordinary sized home-
made cake was scoffed at one meal, so we only had cake on
a Sunday. Our mother would sometimes make a chocolate
cake by just adding cocoa, or caraway seed for a seedy cake,
because she had no fruit to put in it. When it was a seed

Village Christmases

Mollie's mother, Blanche, c. 1903

one my elder brothers would start whistling, like birds, and
we younger ones would chant:

> Mother made a seedy cake
> Give us all the belly-ache.

'Course it didn't really give us the belly-ache, and we
most likely got a cuff for saying belly: we often made up jin-
gles and rhymes about a lot of things.

But one of our mother's extravagances was tea. At any
time of the day if folk called, and *if* she'd got some tea in the
caddy, it was always, 'should you like a cup of tea, the kettle
is boiling on the hob?' Our stepfather would grumble, and

say that her insides must be like a pot-boy's apron, but she
would just remind him of what Mr Gladstone said of tea:

> If you are cold, tea will warm you,
> If you are heated, it will cool you.
> If you are depressed, it will cheer you,
> If you are excited, it will calm you.

And that, she said, was a darned good excuse for anybody 'cos
you're bound to suffer from one of those things. After all, there
weren't many treats in those days and a cup of tea — providing
we'd got cups with handles on — and a chat, was quite a luxury
for ordinary people. We, it seems, were always suffering from
chipped and handleless cups (I've learned since that the more
you pay for crocks the longer they last, and they don't chip or
crack so easily), but if a relation was expected, a quickly-
whispered message to one of us children sent us scurrying up to
Mrs Townsend 'up the back', to borrow a couple of cups and
saucers — and woe betide us if we happened to drop and break
one when we took them back up the rough garden path.

While I was writing down my memories, several people
came up and asked me about my next book, and when I
told them it was about Christmases past, some about my
extreme youth, they nearly all piped up with a special one
that they remembered. A few were worth a mention, so I
have included them.

But hard-up as we were, we were – on the whole – very happy. We must have been to remember so much. There was a wonderful community spirit among us, and neighbours were good humoured and kind, continually helping each other out.

Then, gradually, over the years things began to get better for most people. Better working conditions and pay, and better living conditions at home. But for me the struggle to better ourselves, and the memories of those hard-up happy days, will stay with me, vivid and real, for the rest of my life.

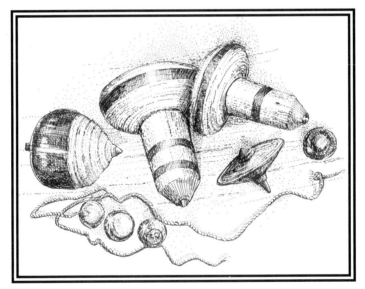

Spinning tops

The Way We Were: Christmas in the Late Twenties

It was Christmas Eve and Mick, my half-sister and I, had been packed off to bed early. My elder sister, Betty, had been left in charge of us. My mother and stepfather had walked up to the nearby town of Witney to buy things for Christmas. You see, my stepfather didn't get paid until five o'clock on Christmas Eve, and with seven children to feed and he only earning two pounds a week, my mother had no chance to buy much before the great day. True, the Christmas puddings had been made about two weeks before, and that was after a great effort: not being able to afford to buy the ingredients all at once, but by buying currants one week and sultanas the next, and so on, until she had all that was needed. Only then could she mix up the puddings – four of them in two-pound pudding basins. Then they were boiled all day long in the washing copper out in the shed, with her renewing the water constantly from the well in the garden.

Village Christmases

Two rabbits, sent through the post from our relations at Sherborne, just a label tied to their feet – no wrapping at all – hung in the back kitchen. They still had to be skinned and gutted. Then, on Christmas Day, the fire in the living room would be made up, red hot ashes poked under the old oven to get it good and hot. Then our mother would stuff the rabbits' bellies with stuffing made of breadcrumbs, parsley, thyme (from our garden) and a good big onion; then she'd lay them in the roasting tin surrounded by pounds of potatoes and covered in dripping, and bake them for about two hours or more (full recipe for baked rabbit on pages 77–8). A separate tin of potatoes was also put in; with nine mouths to feed, 'taters' were a good filler, and my elder brothers were growing up fast – my mother used to say 'I reckon they got hollow legs', for they were always hungry.

Christmas and all that we hoped to get was all that Mick and I talked about as we lay in bed. We had each hung up one of our mother's black stockings on the brass knob of the bedstead. We always planned to stay awake until our parents came home, but, as ever, we fell asleep only to wake very early on Christmas morning to find the knobbly filled stockings. When I say 'filled' I mean that our parents, home from the town, had then turned round and put in as much as they could afford. The contents were nearly always the same – an orange, wrapped in orange tissue paper, which we carefully smoothed out – this was then used when we went

Stocking fillers

to the lavatory, as it was a nice change from the usual 'bum fodder' that we had to use – old newspapers and catalogues. Then always a nice rosy apple, a screw of nuts wrapped in newspaper, along with a screw of dates similarly wrapped; a pink sugar mouse with a string tail and a chocolate watch wrapped in silver paper. A painting book or a slim reading book in the leg of the stocking completed our Christmas treat. We stuffed ourselves with the orange, apple, nuts and dates before getting up. Squeals of delight were coming from our parents' bedroom (there were only two bedrooms in the cottage and a big landing), where the two youngest, Ben and Denis, slept. They still believed in Father Christmas,

Mollie's sister, Betty, 1929

and Mick and I, and indeed my older sister and brothers, Betty, Bunt and Bern, were dared to let on to them that it was all a fairy story. When I came home years past, bawling my head off because Sidney Edgington had told me that it was 'yer Mum and Dad what fills yer stocking', I tried not to believe him, but in my heart I knew this was so.

So our mother took me on her lap and said, 'It's Father Christmas as long as you believe, then as soon as you dis-believe then it has to be your parents who fill your stocking.' 'But,' she went on, 'don't you dare tell Mick, or Ben or Denis.' Anyhow, it wasn't long before someone had told Mick – but thankfully, at this very moment, for young Ben and Denis, it was still the magic of Father Christmas.

VILLAGE CHRISTMASES

I told my son the same story and later on my grandsons, when older children also told them, 'It's your mother and father what fills your stockings.'

Gradually the rest of the family woke up, and we all trailed down to breakfast. No change here: porridge with lashings of skimmed milk, then there was the washing-up to do, and the stairs to dust – my daily job. Then the painting book was soon filled, and we just waited for dinner.

The day before we had made paper-chains with paper cut from any coloured food packets – mostly tea. After we'd cut the strips of paper we then stuck them together with home-made flour paste (of just flour and water), then pinned them up all over the living room. A few bits of holly and ivy over the pictures, and that was the Christmas decorations (Christmas trees for the cottagers were unheard of – but we always had a big one at the school Christmas treat). The treat was given by Major and The Hon. Mrs Feilden of Cokethorpe House – a big country mansion just outside the village of Ducklington. The tree, massive it was, touched the ceiling of the schoolroom – it came from their estate at Cokethorpe Park. The tree was beautifully decorated with nightlights in little coloured glass jars hanging from the branches (in earlier years it was lit with candles fixed into 'pinch-on' candlesticks) and there was a beautiful fairy on the topmost branch. There was a present on there for every child in the school. We had a lovely tea, with plates of

Ducklington schoolchildren sliding on the pond outside the school, 1940

wafer-thin bread and butter, such as we never had at home. Then there was seedy cake and currant cake – made by the local baker, Mr Collis, and gallons of strong tea. Once I slipped a slice of cake in my frock pocket to take home for my mum. But in the excitement of the games that we played afterwards, it was nothing but a crumbly mess when I got home.

Weeks before we had sat in the evenings and made presents for our mother. Busy with French knitting (with any bits of wool we could get hold of) we made little mats for her to stand her geranium pots on, or a knitted iron-holder or

kettle-holder. My stepfather always bought my mum a bottle of Stone's ginger wine, and that was about it – but
although there was never any money to do anything else,
there was always plenty of home-made wine, which we
drank like water. Some folks might have thought in those
hard-up times that making home-made wine was a bit
extravagant. But our mother, like her parents, believed that
as well as being a cheap, pleasant drink most home-made
wines had medicinal properties. Things gradually got a bit
better as the years went by, with my eldest brothers at work
and later, sister Betty, but it's the early hard-up Christmases
that I remember most. The other memorable Christmas was
the one I spent with my grandparents at Sherborne – but
that's another story!

As I Remembered

FROM MRS LILY BRIDGEWATER

This happened one year at the school Christmas treat, held
in the village school and given by the Feildens.

*One year, Eva Edwards was asked to play Father Christmas and
give out the presents to us children, off the Christmas tree. She was
a tall, well-built girl so I suppose that was why she was chosen to
be Father Christmas. Anyhow, before giving out the presents she
was asked to light the candles on the tree. Unfortunately, she started
to light the ones nearest to her, and as she bent over to light some of
the others further away, her cotton wool beard set alight.
I can't remember who put it out, but there was an awful scuffle for
a few minutes.*

The Way We Did French Knitting

Most children, when I was young, knew how to do French knitting.

It was a good way of using up any odd bits of wool, and of keeping youngsters quiet. And what we made from the knitting was useful anyway. The most popular things was to make little mats – round or oval – for parents to stand flower pots on, but kettle-holders and iron-holders were also made. Another very handy thing was to make babies' reins, and I remember when my son, Peter, was beginning to walk, I made some for him – sewing little bells on, to help make it a bit more like the real bought ones.

French knitting is very simple to do. All you need is a wooden cotton reel and four tin-tacks and, of course, an endless supply of oddments of wool. When we were small we longed for our mother to finish using the cotton on a reel so that we might use the reel to make something for her for Christmas. You will see by the picture how to hammer the tacks into the top end of the cotton reel, then you

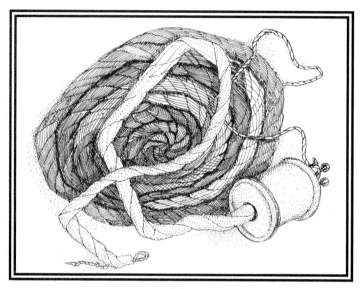

French knitting

simply set on four stitches, one on each tack, but be sure and leave a 'tail' which you poke through the reel – this gives you something to gently pull the knitting through as you do it. And it is just like an ordinary knitting stitch, looping the one on the tin tack over with wool each time, with the aid of a pin or large needle. That's all there is to it. You knit as long or short as you wish, also casting off as you would ordinary knitting. If you are making mats, or iron-holders, you simply sew the long tube of knitting up to whatever shape you want. For children it is quite an achievement, much better for them than giving them the money to purchase ready-made things.

Christmas Party

FROM AGNES NEILAND

It's strange, but the only thing that sticks in the minds of the folk who I went to school with at Ducklington so long ago, and those who followed for years afterwards, was the Christmas party given by the Feildens: this is what Agnes Neiland told me.

As Christmas approached, we children looked forward to the party given by Mrs Feilden (by this time I think that probably Major Feilden had died), from Cokethorpe House. The party was held in the parish room. My sister and I would set off in new dresses which were part of – or totally – our Christmas present. Mrs Feilden was, I remember, a grey-haired lady with twinkling eyes. She was helped by Mrs Peel from the Manor and some of Mrs Feilden's maids from Cokethorpe House. We enjoyed a plentiful tea, and games of musical chairs, etc. afterwards. Then later, parents were invited and we children sang or recited – according to our nerve and talent. Then we returned home, clutching a bag with an orange, a mince-pie and sweets.
They were wonderful parties and really the only one that we had at Christmas-time.

Ducklington and Hardwick Women's Institute. The Hon. Mrs Feilden is sitting
in the middle of the second row (flower in lapel)

The Making of our Christmas Puddings

It was a great event in our house, the making of the Christmas puddings. Mind you, the collecting of the ingredients had started weeks before, a bit at a time just when my mother could manage it: half the time mother never knew where the next copper was coming from. So, the collecting for the Christmas puddings was a marathon job, a pound of currants one week and perhaps raisins the next. Mind you, during this period of collecting our mother might suddenly deside to make a 'spotted dick' (boiled suet pudding with currants in) for our dinner. But no currants could be found in our old larder, so she'd 'borrow' some of her Christmas collection, which were carefully stored in her old red earthenware pan – whether they were ever replaced was another matter. Anyhow, try as she would she very rarely got all the stuff together by 'Stir-up Sunday' – the first Sunday in Advent: this was when folk said that you should have made and boiled your puddings; others said that if the pudding were made

by 'Stir-up Sunday', the Lord's blessing would be on all
who tasted the puddings. 'Course, we believed in the
jingle:

> Stir up, we beseech thee,
> The pudding in the pot,
> And when we all gets hungry,
> We'll eat the blummen lot.

But in the Book of Common Prayer, the wording is very
different:

> Stir up, we beseech Thee, O Lord, the wills of Thy
> faithful people; that they plenteously bringing forth
> fruit of good works, may be of Thee plenteously rewarded.

But then we parodied most things, like the carol 'While
Shepherds watched' – our version of this was:

> While shepherds watched their dirty socks,
> A-boiling in the pot,
> A lump of soot came tumbling down,
> And spoilt the blummen lot.

Some sang while shepherds *washed* their flocks by night
believing that they were singing the right words! And others

sang, 'While shepherds *washed* their dirty socks . . .'. But I heard my brothers singing a different version: 'While shepherds watched their turnip tops a-boiling in the pot . . .'.

Never mind the old wives' tale, 'Never wash clothes on Christmas Day or New Year's Day – lest you should wash your soul away.'

We also sang other versions of 'Hark the Herald Angels sing':

> Hark the Herald Angels sing,
> Beecham's Pills are just the thing.
> One for men, two for women,
> Half for children
> Under seven.
> If you want to go to heaven,
> You must take about six or seven.
> Hark the Herald Angels sing,
> Beecham's Pills are just the thing.

(If that's the case I shall prefer to go to the Other Place, remembering from my childhood what havoc two Beecham's used to play to the old stomach on Friday nights: we were up and down to that old privy forty-thousand times!)

and

> Hark the Herald Angels sing,
> Beecham's pills are a very good thing,
> Keeps your innards meek and mild,
> Two for a man and one for a child.

then there was the carol singers' chant:

> Knock on the knocker,
> Ring on the bell,
> If you don't give us a penny,
> You'll end up in Hell.

It is believed that the origin of bringing greenery into the house at Christmas-time stems from a pagan custom of welcoming the wood spirits into the shelter and warmth of people's dwelling places, and I also remember this rhyme; we used to chant

> Ink, pink, pen and ink,
> Who made the awful stink,
> The blackie man said it was you,
> So out of the room you must go,
> Because the King and Queen said so.

But if our mother heard us singing these parodies of carols she'd give us a clout: blaspheming, she'd say it was, or taking the Lord's name in vain.

Anyhow, our Christmas puddings, more often than not, were most likely mixed and cooked about two weeks before Christmas and were the loveliest puddings I've ever tasted. I have always used our mother's recipe, and the puddings are always fine – but somehow they never taste quite so lovely as hers did, perhaps it is because these days we are not as hungry as we were then. In those days raisins came with their stones in; that was mine and Mick's job to stone them, a horrible messy job it was too.

We'd sit at the scrubbed table, with a basin of water near at hand, so that our sticky fingers could be dipped in now and then. Otherwise, after you'd taken the stones from the fruit, they simply stuck to your fingers. Our stepfather who worked at the local brewery always brought a quart of old beer to mix the puddings with. The mixture was never put in the basins until every member of the family had had a stir and a wish. My own pet theory of stirring the puddings is nothing to do with the wishing bit. I think that, years ago, some wise old woman thought of this as a way to get her puddings well and truly mixed, and the wishing part was added to make it a bit more of an event. Anyhow, I'm very glad when my family come and stir mine: that mixture is a bit thick and heavy – think of someone with a weak wrist!

VILLAGE CHRISTMASES

But really I like to believe this theory, that the mixture should always be stirred with a wooden spoon, in memory of the wooden manger where the baby Jesus slept; and also stirred three times – from east to west – in memory of the three kings who came from the East to bring gifts to the Christ child.

Then there was the putting of threepenny bits in with the mixture: was this, I wonder, to make you eat your portion slowly? I still have two Victorian threepenny pieces that belonged to my gran, which she used to put in her puddings – always asking for them back after they'd been found in the rich pudding. I supposed she couldn't afford to give them away. I also have two very tiny white porcelain figures – a boy and a girl. They were given to me years ago by an elderly neighbour. She told me her mother always put them in their Christmas puddings (they never had money in theirs), and the ones who found them would be lucky all the next year. Again, these had to be handed back to enable them to go in the puddings the next Christmas-time.

Here is the recipe which my mother and I have always used when making our puddings. Breadcrumbs were used, no flour at all – making the puddings much lighter and crumbly:

MY MOTHER'S CHRISTMAS PUDDING

*3/4 lb fine breadcrumbs (these can be all white, a mixture of
brown and white, or all brown)*

1/2 lb raisins

1/2 lb currants

1/2 lb sultanas

1/2 lb suet

4 oz chopped mixed peel

1 grated carrot

1/2 lb soft brown sugar

1 1/2 oz blanched finely chopped almonds

1/2 juice and grated rind of a lemon

1/2 heaped teaspoon nutmeg

1/2 teaspoon salt

2 teaspoons mixed spice

4 large eggs

1/2 pint old beer or stout

METHOD: Stir all the ingredients together well (with
the help of the family). If you think it is not quite wet
enough, add a little milk. Pour the mixture into well
greased basins, cover and tie tightly down, first with
greaseproof and then (these days) with foil. Boil for 6 to
8 hours. Take the covers off as soon as possible and leave

19

the puddings to DRY OUT WELL, before covering them with clean dry paper.

Store in a cool place and boil for a further two hours on the day that you eat them.

There was the year when Mrs Hathaway, who lived in the Square at Ducklington, cooked her Christmas puddings nice and early, and duly tied nice clean cloths over them, and set them up on a high shelf in the kitchen. They were a biggish family and she had made eight lovely puddings, the first to be eaten on Christmas Day, and one on each Sunday afterwards until they were all gone.

Early Christmas morning she climbed up on to her stool

The Square, Ducklington

to get one. The first basin was empty, although the cloth was still tied on neatly. She reached for the next – and that was empty too. And so were all the rest!

The culprits were two of her elder sons. They used to come in at night after the others had gone to bed, and over the weeks had completely eaten the half-cooked puddings!

Legend has it that there should be thirteen ingredients in your Christmas puddings, in memory of Christ and his twelve disciples; and finely chopped mutton suet in your mince pies in memory of the shepherds.

A Winter Journey to the Cotswolds

Near one Christmas, about a year after our mother had married our stepfather, she said that she wanted her mother and father – our gran and gramp – to meet him. As our own father had tragically died just about two months before I was born, I, of course – during those lonely struggling years for our mother – had been made a real fuss of, and probably rather spoilt, and no doubt resented the affection which our mother bestowed on our stepfather. Not that I wasn't loved, I was, but not quite in the same way.

But now I was about four years old, and my elder brothers, Bern and Bunt, and my sister Betty, were about eight, seven and six respectively. Well, arrangements were made that our stepfather would borrow Mr Midwinter's pony and trap and drive us all, one Saturday, to Sherborne in the Cotswolds.

It was a cold wintry morning when we set off. There was a strong north wind blowing, which our mother said was coming straight from Siberia.

Mollie's father, Fred Woodley, who died two months before Mollie was born

VILLAGE CHRISTMASES

This is the sort of pony and trap that Mollie travelled to Sherborne in

We children were all wrapped up warm, with scarves tied over our hats and round our ears, across our chests and tied at the back. Our stepfather had on his old army greatcoat so he must have been nice and warm. But I remember our mother looked cold as we drove along. Good job that Mr Midwinter had put some hay on the floor of the trap – this helped to keep our feet warm. We had a few little presents for our grandparents – just things that we had made, little

*Granny Broad with eldest son (Uncle Will)
and Mollie's mother*

mats for gran to put her pots of geraniums on. One thing I
remember vividly about our gran, she always had a window-
sill full of bright red geraniums. We'd also made her an iron-
holder and kettle-holder, and our mother had knitted a pair
of thick warm mittens for our gramp. In a box there was
one of our mother's Christmas puddings, and a bottle of
home-made wine – but gran always made plenty anyway,
and our mother said that hers was probably not as good as
Granny Broad's. Our mother had also packed a crusty loaf
and a pot of jam to help out: six extra mouths to feed would
be rather a lot for Granny Broad to find.

Our stepfather took the valley road; he said it wouldn't be
so cold and windy as the top road (now the A40). There was

little or no traffic in the villages that we passed through; just occasionally he had to pull the pony and trap on to the grass verge to let a farm wagon go by, on those narrow village roads by Asthall, Swinbrook and Fulbrook, coming to Burford bridge, and on to Taynton and the Barringtons. Our stepfather pulled up at The Fox at Little Barrington, where he bought himself a half pint of beer and brought out a bottle of lemonade for us. I remember the bottle had a glass marble in, and I cried because I couldn't get it out. We scrambled down from the trap, stiff and cold. Then we all had a swig at the lemonade, taking it in turns so that the bottle was soon empty. 'Alright,' our stepfather said, 'get back up and take your seats.'

Then we set out for the village of Windrush, and then on to Sherborne. The sky was blue-black with snow clouds and our stepfather crossed his arms and banged his hands across his chest to warm them. I found out later that this action was called 'Baffam Jack'.

A few flakes of snow began fithering down and we children huddled closer together for warmth. 'Shan't be long now', our mother assured us. We passed through the village of Windrush where some girls were skipping – they stopped their game and gazed at us as we passed, one of them poking her tongue out. They – and a horse and dung cart that came along – were about all that we saw. 'Only a few more miles', our mother had said smilingly, but here our stepfather left

Sherborne. This picture is very much how Mollie remembers the village

the valley and made for the Northleach/Cheltenham road, for it was on this road that gran and gramp's lodge was situated, one of a pair at the entrance to Sherborne Park and mansion, the home of Lord and Lady Sherborne. My gran was paid sixpence a week to open and shut those great wrought-iron gates every time anyone or anything came and went back through them.

At last we reached the lodge. Our gran was standing at the door waiting for us. She had heard the pony

The lodge on the left where Mollie's grandparents lived at Sherborne Park

clip-clopping along – there was little or no other traffic on the road. Gran was dressed in a long black dress buttoned high at the neck, a long white apron, and a crocheted shawl over her shoulders.

We tumbled out of the trap like a nest full of young birds. Granny kissed our mother and each of us children in turn. Then she turned to our stepfather – a handsome young man with laughing eyes. 'So you be he, then?' she said, and shook his hand. 'Grampy is still at work, but he'll soon be home for his vittals,' she said.

We trooped into the lodge, which was a single-storey building. It was lovely and warm in the living room with a good fire burning. Saucepans were steaming and boiling on the hobs. 'I've got you a bit of dinner ready', Gran said, and we children were sat up at that table in a flash, waiting. 'But it's only half-past eleven!', our mother said.

'Never mind,' Gran replied, 'I'll bet you be all starving hungry', and she ladled out hot rabbit stew with lots of veg-etables, and it was lovely.

'I'll cut some bread,' our mother said, 'help fill them up', and we sobbled the gravy up with the bread that she had brought from home. Then Gran fetched out a big steaming roly-poly pudding from one of the big black saucepans. She carefully took the hot cloth off it, and slipped it on to the dish – it looked like a picture of a zeppelin I'd seen, round and long. A lovely jam roly-poly it was, and we soon scoffed our helpings, and looked hopefully for more. Gran noticed our looks. 'That bit what's left is for your gramp, he'll be fair famished when he gets back – out in this cold weather', and she slipped the last remaining slice on to a plate, and put it in the fire oven to keep warm. Our stepfather said that he'd better go and give the pony his food, 'and cover him up too', he added.

Our mother and gran cleared the dirty plates up and took them out to the little scullery, and washed them up using a kettle of hot water from the hob to do it. We could hear them chattering – our mother was probably telling Gran

The shirt-sleeved man could easily be Grampy Broad as he is listed in the latest book on Sherborne by Sybil Longhurst as Shepherd Broad who, in 1911, was earning 14s a week there

what a lovely man our stepfather was (and he was, too), first to take us children on – there were four of us – and secondly to work hard to keep us in food and clothes. But he was also a happy man, who sang and whistled a lot and often made us laugh.

By now it was snowing very hard, with the wind lashing it against the window panes.

Ben Butler, Mollie's stepfather, is on the right

Our grampy came home at last, stamping his boots to get the snow off. 'You could have chosen a better day, I reckon', he said as he said 'hello' to our stepfather. 'Looks as if we be in fer a deep 'un', he added. Then he gave us each a hug and a kiss in turn. Our mother came out of the scullery and threw her arms around him. She loved her father very much. 'It's good to see you looking so well and happy', he said as he took his jacket off, and hung it up to dry.

Gran put his dinner out: ''tent as much as it should a-bin, but them young rascals was fair famished', she told him. And he, too, was glad of some bread, 'to fill the corners up', he told us, his eyes twinkling with delight to see us.

After a while our stepfather said, 'well, I think we shall

have to soon make a move. I'll go and fetch the trap round.'
He opened the door and shut it up again quickly: the snow
was two to three feet deep and already half way up the door.

'Whatever shall we do?' our mother cried.

'Well, we can't go in this, that's for sure', our stepfather
replied.

Gramp said, 'Then you'd best take that pony and shut
him in the out-house, and try and cover the trap up with
these sacks', pulling a bundle from the corner of the room.
'But before you goes, we'll make you summut to go over
your head and shoulders', Gramp said.

Taking a good big sack in his hand he turned it up so that
the bottom of the sack was in his hand, and then he folded
it in half. Then he took hold of one corner and pushed it
into the other corner, making a sort of hood and cape like a
monk's hood. 'Thur you be', he said. 'All the farm workers
wears 'um in this sort of weather', and he slipped it on to
our stepfather's head, tying it round his neck with a piece of
bag-tie string – and then he trudged off, head down battling
against the storm, to shut the pony in the dry. Our stepfather was gone quite a long time, and when he came back
he was covered, like a snowman. 'You'd best get them boots
off quick, or you'll be 'ett up with the rhematics', Gran said.
'You'll just have to stay the night, Blanche', she went on,
seeing our mother's worried look. 'We'll manage somehow,
we got plenty of grub; thurs a side of bacon hung up, and

I'll soon rasher some of that off, and the hens be laying well – we shan't starve ourselves, that's fer sure.'

Of course, at the time we children didn't realise how serious the situation was, and what a lot of work feeding and sleeping six extra souls would make, and we were very excited to think that we were all going to stay at Gran's for the night.

Then Gramp said he ought to go and see that the pig and chickens were alright, with food, water and bedding, and he dressed himself up, putting a folded sack – like he'd made for our stepfather – over his head and shoulders, and went out to weather the storm. Our mother and gran were busying about and fetching out blankets, rugs and pillows and airing them in front of the fire. There were only two rooms in the lodge, so I expect there was a bit of juggling that went on to sleep us all. In the end, we four children slept in the small second bedroom in a single bed, we two girls at the top and Bern and Bunt at the bottom, our feet meeting in the middle of the bed. There was much squealing, laughing and tugging of the bed-clothes before our mother came in, very annoyed, and chastised us for behaving so badly. She took the lighted candle away, telling us to go to sleep or we'd all have a slap. I never did know what the other sleeping arrangements were, and we children must have all slept well for it was daylight before any of us stirred. There was a lovely smell of home-cured fried bacon wafting through, and we

all squittered out of bed and soon dressed – well, there
wasn't much to put on! Betty and I had had to sleep in our
vests and knickers, and the boys in their shirts. Luckily there
had been a bit of a thaw overnight, and our stepfather said
he thought that the road – if we kept to the top one –
would be passable, and he went out to fetch the pony and
trap round.

After a good breakfast of bacon and egg and crispy fried
bread, we sadly had to say goodbye to our gran – Grampy
had already left for work before we woke up. Gran packed
us up some seedy cake and some bread and jam, and a bottle
of cold tea. We piled into the trap, Gran giving us a rosy rug
to wrap our legs in. We had that rug for years – it was simply a couple of old thin blankets sewn together, and the
whole thing covered in rosy crettone. If we were ill, our
mother would say, 'I'll wrap you in Gran's rosy rug' – that
seemed to cure 'most everything. Time to go, with lots of
hugs and kisses from Gran, and we settled ourselves in the
trap. Our stepfather clicked his tongue, and said to the pony,
'Righto, Dolly, let's head for home'. We kept waving goodbye, and calling Happy Christmas to Gran until there was a
bend in the road and we could see her no more.

It had stopped snowing and there were a few marks in the
road where carts had gone along, but we almost got stuck
several times. Then our stepfather would hand our mother
the reins and he'd jump down, sometimes up to his knees in

A snowy day in Eynsham

Deep and crisp and even

snow, and push the trap from behind. He was a strong man and would soon get us going again. And other times he would get out and lead the pony if the snow was not quite so deep. We stopped once on the way back at a pub where our stepfather had a half pint of beer. He also cadged some oats for the pony, in a nosebag which he fixed over the pony's head, and Dolly was soon tossing that nosebag up to get to the bottom of it and the last of the oats. We had a drink of cold tea and it was lovely, and we tucked into the bread and jam and seedy cake until it was all gone. Soon we passed the turning to Burford, but kept to the main road for the rest of the journey. Our mother started singing, and we all joined in, with our stepfather singing us cheeky wartime songs 'Inky Pinky Parla vou Charlie Chaplins got the flue'. This helped to make the time go quicker, and soon we turned off the main road for Ducklington. And we were all glad to get home.

First the dog, cat, the hens and pig had to be fed as they had been without grub for nearly twenty-four hours. The pig with his head and his front feet on the top rail of his sty, squealed like billy-o until he was fed. But none of them was any the worse for their untimely fast. Our mother soon got the fire going and the kettle boiling, and we all sat down to a cup of strong sweet tea. Then our stepfather had to take the pony and trap back up to Witney to Mr Midwinter, who, of course, was very pleased to see him, with no harm having been done to the trap or to Dolly. There was a parcel of Christmas presents from our gran and gramp, which turned out to be hand-knitted gloves for us all. And we children never stopped talking about the exciting weekend when we got snowed up at our grandparents in the Cotswolds.

PS: The reason why the journey for a four-year-old is still so vivid, is because for years it was told and retold, over and over again, to all our friends and relations. You see, there were not many folk in those days who got snowed up and had to spend the night miles and miles away from home.

The Pictures from the Fire

FROM KEN STOUT, NOW LIVING IN POOLE

*My first memory of Christmas was one I spent with my
grandparents: I was about four years old at the time. They had this
huge open fire with seats at the sides, and a big black iron fireback
attached to the wall at the back of the fireplace where a lot of soot
seemed to collect. We sat there one Christmas Day – me on my
Gramp's lap – snoozing, and also now and then watching the
pictures in the fire. On one of his wakeable moments my
grandfather said, 'Never mind the pictures in the fire, look at the
ones on the fireback'. The flames from the fire had sort of caught
light to the particles of soot which ran up and down that old
fireback. 'See,' he said, pointing to the runnets of sparkling soot,
'see, that's all the people walking up the winding path to Church.'
And then a little later on he pointed to another line of lighted soot
fragments on the fireback, and said, 'And that's them all going back
home again!' I've never forgotten it. Funny, it's the only thing I
remember about my Grampy.*

Cotswold Days

After our adventures just before Christmas a couple of years before, when we had to stay overnight at Granny Broad's, our stepfather said that he would take us to Sherborne again – come the better weather. We children didn't let him forget his promise to us, and we kept badgering him until at last he agreed that 'come Saturday, we'll go', and, he said, 'that's if Mr Midwinter will lend us the pony and trap again'.

So that was it. One lovely June morning we set off, the weather was beautiful, the sun warm on our backs as we journeyed along the top road (now the A40). It was clear, and we could see for miles and miles, and our mother kept pointing out places of interest to us. The time seemed to pass quickly and we soon left Witney, and then Burford behind us. We came to The New Inn (now called An Inn for All Seasons), and our stepfather tied the pony up under a tree and went inside for a drink. We sat outside in the trap and drank ginger beer that our mother had made from one of those ginger beer plants that she kept on the window-sill at home. The liquid had to be fed every day with a teaspoon

'Those were the days.' A scene in Bridge Street, Witney

of sugar and one of ground ginger. If you forgot – which our mother did quite often – the plant died, and that meant starting all over again. Then she would shout, 'Go on, take a jam-jar and call at Mrs Tremlin's, and ask her if she has got a ginger beer plant that she can let me have.' And Betty and I would go squittering down the village to the Tremlins' house, and make our request to the old lady.

'What!', she would cry, 'I never see such a person as your mother for letting her ginger beer plants die. I giv' her one only a couple of weeks ago. You tell her to look after it proper this time', she called to us as we slunk back up her garden path.

But when our mother did remember to feed the demand-
ing plant it made the most lovely refreshing drink: it was
sweet and fizzy, and once one of the full bottles exploded,
shooting glass and ginger beer all over the place . . .

Our stepfather came out of the inn, smacking his lips and
wiping his mouth. He had enjoyed his half-pint – all that he
could afford with his ready-made family.

We set off again, arriving at our grandparents' home about
midday. Gran had a meal ready for us – lovely rabbit pie it was.
I can't remember what vegetables we had, but there was a big
dish of lovely red plums and custard for our pudding.

After a little while we piled into the trap again and made
the short journey down into the village to the little farm
where our mother's brother, Uncle Will, and his wife,
Auntie Sarah, and their three children – our cousins Bill,
Arnold and Mabel – lived.

We all settled in the living room, chattering nineteen to
the dozen. Then I realised that our mother was talking
about me. 'The trouble is,' she went on, 'I suppose we
spoiled her a bit, her being the youngest, and the fact that
she never even saw her father.'

'Ah, I expect she's had her nose put out', my Auntie
Sarah said, looking at our stepfather.

Then, because they were whispering, I couldn't quite
catch what they were saying, but I did hear our mother say,
'Yes, sometime in November.' I couldn't imagine what

Auntie Sarah, Uncle Will and cousins at Sherborne

could be happening all that while away – after all it was only June. Then Auntie Sarah said, 'Why not let her stay here for a bit; a change might do the little maid a bit of good'.

But instead of being happy at the thought of staying at their little farm for a few weeks, I felt jealous and angry – that was my trouble! I was jealous of our jolly, laughing, stepfather, and my parents thought a short break away from the family might cure me.

I watched them go trotting off down the dusty road. They all waved goodbye, and our mother called, 'now you just be a good girl, and we will come back for you very soon'.

A country lane in Sherborne

Once they were out of sight I stormed and raged and shut myself in the privy down the bottom of the garden, and refused to come out. Then I killed several bluebottle flies that came buzzing in on that hot sultry afternoon. After a while my cousin, Mabel, who was about eight years older than me, came to see if she could entice me out.

'Come on,' she cried, 'come on out, and I'll take you for a walk. I know a secret way to reach the old windmill. We won't let on to nobody where we're going.'

The offer sounded tempting, and I eagerly left my sanctuary.

She took my hand and we walked over hundreds and hundreds of fields – well, it seemed like hundreds to me! But the windmill standing up there on the skyline seemed further away than ever.

'How much further?' I cried.

'We shall soon be there', my cousin said.

But I was hot and tired and sat down in the middle of a field and bawled my head off. I took off my boots and threw my bunch of wild flowers away – they were drooping anyway – and refused to walk another step.

I said that we were lost and that nobody would ever find us. My cousin sat down beside me and she, too, was crying, wiping her hot streaming face on her white lace edged petticoat.

Suddenly we heard voices shouting our names urgently; there were people running across the field towards us. It was my uncle and cousins who had been searching for us for hours.

'Thank God you're safe!' I heard Uncle Will cry, as he gathered me up in his hot sweaty sunburned arms. We had walked over six miles across those fields, crossing Sherborne brook on a narrow footbridge. We had been gone five hours and we still hadn't reached the windmill.

Later that night, as I lay in the coolest, nicest, lavender-smelling sheets that I had ever slept in, my cousin whispered, 'never mind, you and I will go to the windmill one day, when you're bigger'.

VILLAGE CHRISTMASES

Instead of staying with them for a little while, I stayed for nearly a year: summer came and went, then autumn and then winter. I walked backwards and forwards with my cousins to the village school, and hated it, and was a naughty, disobedient girl.

But Christmas with them was quite special, the only part that I enjoyed in my long stay with them. We had helped to make the puddings and a lovely cake which we marzipanned and iced – something that we didn't have at home. Cousin Mabel and I were busy making things and putting up decorations, first making them with coloured paper and flour-paste. Uncle Will had been fattening up a great cockerel and there it hung, dead as dead, out in the outhouse waiting to be plucked and drawn. We were looking forward to our Christmas dinner, and to a party that we – my cousins and I – had been invited to on Boxing Day.

But first it was Christmas Eve, and the hanging up of our stockings – I knew by now that it wasn't old Father Christmas who came and filled them up. I think my Auntie Sarah was trying hard to make it a lovely Christmas for me, being that I was away from home. Mabel and I awoke very early to see what we'd got in our stockings. I had an orange and an apple, nuts and dates, a lovely red hand-knitted jumper – when my auntie had made it I don't know, but I loved it and wore it all the holiday, and it was much admired. There was a parcel from my mother and stepfather

– a sugar mouse, a chocolate Father Christmas and some nice warm stockings, and a long letter wishing me a merry Christmas, and that they would come and fetch me home very soon – which cheered me up no end.

We had a wonderful dinner with lashings of chicken meat, baked potatoes and greens, and afterwards the lovely Christmas pudding and custard that Mabel and I had helped to make. We also drank lots of home-made wine – I think it was blackberry. We, at Sherborne, drank wine every day with our dinner, but we definitely had more on that day, and I felt quite woozy and promptly got on their horse-hair stuffed sofa (which prickled my legs), and slept until tea-time.

Uncle Will and cousins Bill and Arnold went out to feed the animals and milk the three cows, bringing in the lovely warm milk which they poured into big wide pans. One thing I enjoyed while I was there was the lovely butter which Auntie Sarah made, skimming the cream off the milk and then pouring the cream into a small churn, which she hand-turned until it turned into the buttercup yellow butter. That's what we had for our Christmas tea, lots of thin bread spread with this lovely farm butter, and then covered with home-made strawberry jam. Then Auntie cut the decorated cake and it was super! After tea Mabel and I played games – I Spy and Blind Man's Buff – with our cousins, Arnold and Bill, joining in. It was warm and comfy in their living room, and for a while I forgot about being away from home.

Left to right, back: cousins Arnold, Mabel, -?-, Bill; front: Arnold's wife-to-be
Annie and Auntie Sarah

The next afternoon we walked up to a house on the Farmington Road, near the old mill – which a few years later my uncle and aunt moved to. It was cold and frosty and I was glad of my nice new red jumper. I can't remember the people's name, but they were quite well off because it was a nicely furnished home with lovely Christmas decorations in the rooms. There were three or four young girls there, which pleased Bill and Arnold. First, we had a fabulous tea – jelly and blancmange and little iced cakes and sausage rolls. Afterwards we went into their front room and played lots of games. The one I liked best was postman's knock – there was lots of squealing and laughing as the girls and boys went out to the passage, and came back later red-faced and smiling. I was glad when it was my turn to go out, and was kissed quite passionately by cousin Bill – he was about fourteen and very good-looking, and all the girls fell for him.

Too soon it was time to go back. We were each given a bag which held little cakes and sausage rolls, and a lovely skipping rope each for the girls and marbles for the boys. Frost was glistening on the ground. It looked like millions of diamonds as the light from our candle lanterns shone down.

After a few days it was back to school, and the long walk down the village, there and back.

Winter turned into spring, and I was really more fed up than ever, and behaving very badly. One day I was running back from school, crying as usual, when I saw someone coming towards me on a pushbike. In a moment I was in my mother's arms, being smothered with kisses, and hugged very tightly. She had borrowed a pushbike and then she had cycled from Ducklington (eighteen miles each way) to fetch me home. I expect my auntie had written and told her how unhappy I was. I remember the long, uncomfortable ride home on the hard metal carrier on the back of the bicycle – and

School photo: Mollie is standing in the second row, fifth from right, in the dark dress

how I got pins and needles in my feet and legs as they hung down – but at least I was going home.

There was a wonderful surprise waiting for me when I got home. In my absence my mother had produced a new baby, my half-sister Kathleen (Mick), a fat, curly-headed bundle who looked more like a doll. Suddenly my jealousy disappeared. I was a big girl now. I had been miles and miles away from home for almost a year, and I felt quite grown up.

My First Christmas Tree

FROM EDNA SMITH

*I lived with my gran in the little village of South Leigh. She was a
wonderful lady, and I loved her. One Christmas, I suppose I was
about five years old, I came downstairs on Christmas morning, and
she had got me my very first Christmas tree: you see, not many
working folk had that sort of thing then. But it was wonderful. It
was just a branch, spruce I think it was, stuck in some dirt in an
old galvanised bucket, and the only things it had on were twelve
poppies – you know, the ones that are on sale on 11th November.
Where she got them from I never asked, but it was the loveliest,
best, Christmas tree I ever had.*

Ghosts

On winter nights, especially around Christmas-time, when we were all sitting around the fire, our step-father would often tell us tales about the village that he grew up in. It was near Hungerford – Hongerford, as he called it. You see, his dialect was a bit different from ours, and he spoke of 'The Nell' – the canal which ran near where they lived. He also told us about the tutti men who came round on a special day with a ladder, which they put up to the windows of the cottages, kissing all the ladies living in them.

One tale we loved to hear over and over again, although at first we squealed with fright. It was about the ghosts that haunted the road near the row of cottages where my step-father had lived at one time. The row was called 'The Barracks' – probably this was what the buildings had been used for many years before. The story was about two people who were very much in love. She a pretty, shy, country girl, and he a handsome soldier. Suddenly the regiment was ordered overseas as war had broken out, and it departed at once. The soldier vowed to come back to his beloved Mabel as soon as hostilities ceased.

Well, during one of the dreadful battles, news came back to the village that the soldier, along with many more, had been killed – both his legs had been shot off. Mabel was absolutely broken-hearted, nothing comforted her, and one day, soon afterwards, she drowned herself in the canal.

Several years after this tragedy a very weary and worn ragged old man somehow arrived in the village. He was in a little truck thing which he manoeuvred with his rough hands – he was legless. The poor man was demented, and called out to everyone 'Have you seen my Mabel?' over and over again. Then one of the older men remembered who this fellow was, and eventually told him what had happened to Mabel. The next day someone saw a wooden box affair floating on the canal – Bert had joined his beloved Mabel!

After a while the locals seemed to forget about this tragedy, until people started to say that they had seen, in the half light on balmy summer nights, a courting couple strolling along the village street. The girl wore a white rose sprigged muslin dress and the young man was in soldier's uniform. They had their arms entwined around each other and a look of love in their eyes. Each time they were approached by the villagers they simply disappeared.

'Did you ever see them?' we asked, wide-eyed.

'No,' he replied, 'but my mother saw them several times. But then, she had the gift of second sight. If she'd been born a hundred years ago they'd have burnt her as a witch!'

We children couldn't imagine plump Granny Butler ever being thought of as a witch. The only strange thing about her was patches of brown under her nose: you see, she was a great snuff-taker.

'Tell us some more', we'd cry to our stepfather.

But often it was, 'Go on to bed with you, 'tis long past your bedtime'.

Other times he'd sing to us, songs that he'd learnt when he was in the First World War – 'Madamaselle from Armentiers – par la vou', 'Take me back to dear old Blighty', and 'Round the corner behind the tree'. Sometimes they were folk songs, but part of one of these is all that I can remember – I don't know whether it's the verse or the chorus:

Now such kisses and compliments they paid to each
   other,
As they walked arm in arm along the road, like sister and
   brother.
As they walked arm in arm along the road,
'Til they came to a spring,
Then they both sat down together, love,
To hear the nightingale sing.

VILLAGE CHRISTMASES

I think I remember this bit because it reminds me of a soldier and his lass wandering along the quiet lanes on a balmy summer night, many, many years ago.

And they both sat down together, love,
To hear the nightingale sing.

Forbidden Carol Singing

'Twas about three days before Christmas and I suppose I was about seven or eight years old at the time. We'd been busy making the usual little presents; but I wanted to *buy* my mother something. But how? I had no money and not likely to get any: pocket money in our house was unheard of. But while Bern, Bunt and Betty had been allowed to go carol singing with the church choir and were each given two shillings, I was not supposed to go. For one thing my mother said I was too much of a tomboy to be allowed to go into the church choir. So while the other members of the family were chatting about what they were going to spend their money on, I hatched a little plan. I pretended that I wanted to go to the lavatory – to the little house at the bottom of the garden. 'I'm off to the lavatory', I announced.

'I suppose you wants me to take you!' Betty said annoy-ingly.

'No,' I replied, 'I'll go by myself.'

'Thank goodness for that,' she said, ''bout time you grew up.'

I didn't bother to put my coat on; after all the old lavatory was only a quick squitter down the garden path.

But I didn't go there! I ran past Franklins' cottage, next door to us, and out of the gate and onto the road as quick as a flash, and up the back – that's what we called the row of cottages and one biggish house which lay behind our row. No good going to the three cottages where old Mr Hill, the Townsends and widow Mrs Smith lived – they had no more money than we had. No, I was interested in the house, it was quite a big one, where Mr and Mrs Jewell lived. He worked for Holtoms, the flour mill people at the bottom end of the village. Mr Jewell must have been the man in charge of accounts because he used to collect our rent – you see, our cottage belonged to Holtoms.

I reached the Jewells' house. Warm curtains were drawn over the windows, but there was a glow coming from them. I stood by the door – now for it! I piped up with 'Away in a Manger' in my young squeaky voice, singing the carol all through. I stood still for a moment, then I heard footsteps coming towards the door! I panicked! I wasn't supposed to go carol singing. Our mother said it was like begging: Mr Jewell would tell our mother when he came for the rent, and then I should get a clout round the ear, or a good hard slap on my bottom. I turned, and started to run down the path. The door opened, letting out a shaft of light, and a voice shouted, 'It's alright, Mollie, don't run off, come back here'. I turned round and Mr Jewell stood there. Not the dark-suited Mr Jewell that I knew, but tonight he was dressed in a warm cardigan and he had slippers on. Slowly I walked back.

'That was very nice', he said. 'Mrs Jewell and I enjoyed it. Come inside and I'll see if I can find you some pennies.'

At the thought of 'some pennies', I simply danced into their warm tidy house. The room was beautifully decorated with bought paper-chains hung around, and shiny baubles such as I'd never seen before. 'Coo,' I thought, 'they must be rich.' In the corner of the room stood a small Christmas tree gaily decorated with little candles and lots of shiny things; and a bright fire burned in the grate.

I stood there open mouthed. Mrs Jewell, fair and palely dressed, held out her hand to me. 'Come by the fire, young Mollie, you must be frozen. Fancy coming out on a cold night like this without your coat.' She put her arm around me. She smelt lovely.

I blurted out the whole story. 'Nobody knows I've come here; they all thinks I've gone down to the lavatory.' I started crying – he'd tell our mother for sure.

'Now then, dry your eyes', Mrs Jewell said, wiping my tear-stained face with a very white scented handkerchief. 'We'll keep your secret, if that's what you want, won't we?' she said, looking at Mr Jewell.

'But if you gives me some pennies,' I cried, 'I'll have to tell them where I got them from won't I?'

'Yes, *you* tell your mother if you wish, but I'm sure she will understand, especially when you say it's to buy her a Christmas present.'

But it wasn't pennies they gave me, it was a shiny sixpence. I was a millionaire! a whole sixpence! I clutched hold of the money tight for fear of dropping it. Eager to get home I said, 'I'll have to go or they'll wonder where I've got to.' I gabbled 'Goodbye, and thank you', and ran towards the door. Mr Jewell opened it quickly and I was down that path like a streak of lightning. I rushed indoors.

'Where the devil have you been? We were worried to death when Bet couldn't find you. Down to the lavatory indeed!' our mother cried. By now I had held out my hand with the shiny sixpence gleaming in the lamplight.

'Look what I've got.' Then I told them just what I'd done, and they all laughed – and I didn't get a clout, only a cuddle from my mother.

'You've got the nerve of the old Nick,' she said, 'and you want to go to Witney to spend it on a present for me. Alright, off to bed now, but you can go shopping by yourself tomorrow. But no more carol singing, mind!'

Pleased with myself I went off to bed and cuddled up tightly to Mick, who was fast asleep and nice and warm.

We were always taught to say our prayers – our mother being very strict about that. 'Gentle Jesus, meek and mild', I started – but that was all! I dreamed of row upon row of chocolate Father Christmases, all marching up the road to Witney. They wouldn't stop marching, and all I wanted was for one to stop, so that I could buy one for my mother for Christmas.

The next morning, as soon as I'd had my breakfast, I was off all on my own to spend my money. Past the milkman's, up the New Road, over the railway bridge, and then through the Leys and along the Causeway and into the town. Skipping along I soon reached the High Street, where lots of the brightly lit shops were. I was making for a nice little sweetshop – Ovens it was called: they made lovely home-made sweets, all sorts of flavours – mint humbugs and acid drops and lemon – our mother often used to buy a

The Post Office at Ducklington as it used to be

quarter from there. But it wasn't the sweets I was interested in today. The last time I'd come along here with my mother I'd seen some Father Christmases in the window; all wrapped in silver paper they were, so that you could see the outline of the coat and beard and hat and everything. They were marked at 4¹/₂d. *That* was what I planned to buy for my mother. I went into the shop, clutching my precious sixpence.

'Yes, dear?' little Mrs Ovens said, peering over the counter at me.

'I want to buy a 4¹/₂d Father Christmas – it's a present for my mother.'

'Oh, she will be pleased', Mrs Ovens said, carefully putting the Father Christmas in a little white paper bag. 'Now, then, what are you going to do with the rest of the money?' she enquired.

'I don't know yet', I replied, gazing at all the other goodies – sweets and chocolates, liquorice pipes and sherbet dabs, gobstoppers and toffees. I expect Mrs Ovens wondered whenever I was going to make up my mind. I kept looking at the rows of sweets, but I just couldn't decide. Should I spend a whole penny on aniseed balls or buy four gobstoppers – they lasted for ages and you could keep taking them out of your mouth to see what colour they had changed to. I decided on a pen'oth of Blue Bird toffees.

Armed with the Father Christmas and my toffees, I said

goodbye to Mrs Ovens and started off back down the street stuffing the toffees in my mouth, I'd got a ha'penny left. I was getting a bit hungry, so I thought I might buy myself a cake or something. But the shops were all so bright with Christmas goodies that I just dawdled along feasting my eyes on the lovely things. At last I reached Swinburns, the bakers and cake shop. In the window were lovely glass cakestands with white lace doileys on, and arranged on them were piles of scrumptious looking apple and jam slices, cream horns, Banbury cakes and iced buns. Looking at the prices I knew I couldn't buy any of them: then I noticed a plate of rather pale-looking cakes with little holes in the tops. These were marked at $1/2$d each. 'Good,' I thought, 'I'll have one of them.' Boldly, I went in and asked for 'one of them, please' – pointing at the plate. The lady behind the counter smiled as she served me. I handed over my last coin and left quickly: I was anxious to get started on my cake. I took it from the bag and had a good big bite. Coo – it wasn't half tough and it didn't taste very nice either, but I was so hungry that I finished eating before I got to the big church. It was years before I learned that it was a semi-raw crumpet that I had bought!

Now for the long walk home. I got as far as the station bridge, then thought I'd just have a quick look to see if the Father Christmas was alright. Yes, he was still there, sat in the paper bag all fat and shiny. 'I wonder,' I thought, 'would my mother notice if I had a nibble at his wellington boots?' 'No, I'm sure she wouldn't.' I unwrapped the bottom of him and took a bite – that was his boots and a bit of his trousers gone. Quickly I wrapped him up again, and started to run down the New Road, with the chocolate taste still in my mouth. I stopped again, took another look at him: what about eating the bottom of his coat up to the buckle? I took a good big bite. Whoops! I'd even bitten off his sack of toys – there was only his head left. I got as far as the milkman's, but it was no good: I was starving hungry! So I quickly popped his bearded face and hat into my mouth. Then I set off to run the rest of the way home. Goodness knows what my mother would say when I told her that I *did* buy a chocolate Father Christmas, and had eaten it on the way home.

'Well, where is it?' Betty asked.

'Leave her be', my mother said. 'I expect the poor little devil's hungry; she's been gone four hours.'

I went up to my mother. 'I *did* buy you a Father Christmas, but I was so hungry I 'ett him.' They all laughed at me. My mum said that it was alright and I sat at the table, and she fetched out a plate of vegetables from the old fire oven.

'Go on, get that down you,' she said, 'there's the rabbit's head there somewhere.'

'It 'ent fair,' I cried, as I dug into the food, 'I always gets the head and there 'ent hardly any meat on it.'

'Ah', Bern said. 'But there's the brains, you can eat them, you can do with them, 'cos you 'ent got none of yer own', and he threw back his head and laughed. Our mother clouted his ear and told him not to be so horrible. But it *was* true – I always got the head.

Home-made pin cushions

The Candles

FROM MOLLIE'S NEPHEW, JOHN KEMPSON

Well, you know when we were small, we always spent Christmas at Granny Butler's. We were all in her front room and my mum had lit the candles on the Christmas tree. Suddenly, one of the candles started to burn a branch. 'Quick, Stan,' my mum cried to my dad, 'stop that fire!' He put down the pint of beer that he had half drunk, on Gran's sideboard, and stopped the branch from burning any more. Quick as a flash I picked up his half glass of beer and drunk the lot: I was only four at the time! Even quicker, I rushed down the passage in Gran's bungalow and into the lavatory and spewed the lot up!

A Cotswold Christmas

Such excitement there was in our house one Christmas –
well, at least for me – for I was getting ready to go and
stay with my beloved gran and gramp at Sherborne, in the
Cotswolds, just for the festive season. At six o'clock in the
morning I'd got my flannel nightgown and my pinny
packed, and all the little presents we had been busy making
for me to take to the grandparents.

Our mother bundled my two young half-brothers, Ben
and Denis, into the pram, and we set off for Witney where I
was to be put in the capable hands of Mr Groves, the carrier.
I was wearing one of my sister, Betty's, coats that was miles
too long, and it flapped round my legs as I skipped alongside
my mother. She had knitted me an emerald green tammy
with a fluffy bobble on, and my stepfather had made me a
muff from a rabbit's skin that he had cured. It was cold and
frosty and I snuggled my hands deep inside the warm muff,
my new shiny boots squeaking in rhythm as we hurried
along.

I'd been to Sherborne by carrier cart several times before,
but never had it been so crowded as it was on this day. The

The little girl grew up to be Mollie's Granny Broad

inside was stacked high with boxes and bundles and sacks of apples, and there were hares and rabbits hung on the sides, and some chickens in a crate at the back.

It took the carrier ages to get to Burford because he had to call at several of the cottages in the villages that lay along the valley of the Windrush, delivering boxes of groceries and things.

There were two women travelling in the cart, and we chattered and laughed and stamped our feet in the hay that had been put on the floor to help keep our feet warm. I told them where I was going, and all about my grandparents. Round, red-faced country women they were and they sat opposite, listening to me.

'You'd be a mighty fine story-teller', one of them said. 'Never met a child with such an imagination before. 'Ow old did you say you was – nine? My Nellie's going on fer eleven an' 'er can't chatter like you can.'

When they got down from the cart at Asthall, one called back to Mr Groves. 'You 'ang on and I'll bring 'e out a hot drink; you'll both be froze to the marrow betime you gets to Burford.' She brought out hot cocoa and great hunks of bread and fat bacon, and it was lovely.

When Mr Groves went into the cottages to deliver things, I could hear squealing and laughing and he would come out red-faced and beaming. Then I noticed that he'd got a piece of mistletoe tucked into the peak of his cap. 'What have you got that in there for?' I asked him, and he threw back his head and laughed a big, throaty, hearty laugh.

'Comes in very 'andy, do that bit of mistletoe', he replied. But it was years before I realised how handy it must have been.

When we got nearer to Burford, Mr Groves said that I could come out front with him. It was freezing cold and getting dimpsy. He flung a smelly horse rug over my legs. Then, hearing some children carol-singing, he started booming out in his rich voice 'Good King Wenceslas', and I joined in. Even his pony seemed to trot along better for our carolling.

The lamps and candles had been lit in the cottages and Mr Groves kept banging his hands across his chest to warm them – 'Baffam Jack' that's called by country folk. Then he lit the lamps on the cart and they glowed warm and bright, and as the pony's feet hit the stony road they sent out a shower of sparks like the sparklers did on bonfire night.

We dropped down the last hill into Burford – the lights of the town winking and blinking in the gathering gloom. Mr Groves pulled up outside a house and lifted me from the cart – I could hardly walk, my feet and legs were so cold. This was where he lived and we went into the hot, welcoming kitchen. His wife sat by the roaring fire making toast for our tea. They had four or five children, merry curly-headed kids they were too. After tea we sat up at the table and made

paper-chains to decorate the room with. We cut strips of
paper from brightly coloured tea packets, sticking the ends
together with home-made flour paste, like we did at home.

About six o'clock Mr Greig, the baker, called for me. He
was to take me on the last few miles to Sherborne. He lifted
me up the front of his high cart and wrapped me in a couple
of thick coarse flour sacks. He had to deliver bread at three
more villages before we got to my gran's. I was so tired, as
I'd been travelling since twelve o'clock. I kept dropping off
to sleep, but woke with a start every time the baker shouted
'Whoa there, Jinny!' to his pony.

Then he brought me out a cup of hot, home-made wine
from one of the cottages; it smelt sweet and strong. I took a
sip. 'Go on,' he said, 'open your shoulders and let it down,
it'll do you good. It just bin hotted with a hot poker.' I
could feel the red liquid dropping into my stomach and
soon a muzzy feeling crept over me; it was much stronger
wine than my gran's.

Next thing I knew, my gramp was carrying me into the
warm kitchen. My gran took off my shiny new boots and
my long black stockings, and I cried as the life gradually
came back into my frozen limbs. 'Yer Harry,' my gramp said
to the baker, ''ave a jackety 'tater, warms yer 'ands an' fills
yer belly, that's what 'ot 'taters does.' My gran cut open a
steaming potato for me and spread it with home-made lard
– and it was lovely! After a bit, the baker got up to leave and

my gran handed him a bottle of 'me matheglum wine' as she called it, and my gramp gave him a hen pheasant, one of a pair that his employer had given him for Christmas.

Presently my gran said, 'Come on my little maid, you must be tired out – time you went to bed.'

My gramp swung me up in his great arms. 'Have you put that hot brick in the bed, Mother?' he called. And I was slipped into the lavender-smelling sheets. The heat from the brick that had been in the fire oven all day warmed me through and I was soon asleep.

Next morning when I woke, the pale sun was shining on the window. There had been a sharp frost overnight and the panes were covered with frosty forests of Christmas trees, that seemed to glisten with a million fairy lights. I sat up in bed and scratched the frost with my finger nail, then huffed on the pane, making a small clearing.

This was the day before Christmas and my gran had lots to do. I knelt up in a chair by the big white scrubbed table and helped her to prepare the herbs for the stuffing – parsley and thyme, sage and onion. Gleanings from a summer gar-den they were. After picking and carefully drying the sage, parsley and thyme, she had rubbed the fine leaves from the stalks, afterwards storing the leaves in jam jars tied down with brown paper. The onions came from a big thick rope that hung out in the back kitchen. Roping them had been Gramp's job after he had harvested them the previous

Sherborne House, where Mollie's mother was employed for a couple of years as under-housemaid

autumn, and as we chopped and mixed the herbs together the kitchen was filled with lovely, country, stuffingy smells.

We were going to have such a dinner on Christmas Day – that's all we talked about as we plucked the feathers from the bright cock pheasant. I'd never tasted pheasant before – not that my gran and gramp had it often, only when his employer, the old squire, presented each of his workmen with a brace at Christmas-time.

Village Christmases

My gran showed me what she had had from her ladyship. 'Look, my dear', she said, holding up yards of red flannel. 'Make me some good warm petticoats – needs a bit of wool round yer bones in this climate.' There was a pound of tea too, in grey-coloured packets with pictures on them, showing black men and women working in the fields. 'That's where the tea comes from', my gran told me. 'Hundreds and hundreds of miles away where it's ever so hot. So hot that the sun turns everybody black.'

Every housewife whose husband worked on the Sherborne estate had had a present of some red flannel and tea, as well as boots for the children who were still at home.

Every now and then, my gran had to leave what she was doing, and go and open the park gate to let people through to the big house. 'Drat the visitors', she'd say after several interruptions. 'Don't give a body time to settle at nothing.'

My gramp came home from work about five o'clock. He was a giant of a man and he wore trousers that squeaked as he walked. He had leather straps round his legs, just below the knees, which were used to hitch the trousers up so that the bottoms would not get wet and muddy. All farm workers seemed to wear them. His face was the colour of a russet apple and he had a mop of black curly hair which he washed every day, and screwed-up, bright blue eyes. I asked why he screwed his eyes up and he said, 'Ah! Against the pesky old wind out there', nodding in the direction of the hills.

Village Christmases

There was no trouble to get me off to bed that night. My gramp said that he would be sure to see that the fire was out before he came to bed so that Father Christmas wouldn't burn himself when he came down the chimney. Hopefully I hung one of Gran's old stockings on the brass bed knob. Yet I wondered how Father Christmas would know that I was not still at Ducklington.

Next morning, almost before it was light, I crawled to the bottom of the bed. He had been. I could feel the nobbly, filled stocking. It was packed with things – sugar-mice, a liquorice pipe, nuts, an orange and a rosy apple, a painting book, a chocolate watch – like my gramp wore in his weskit pocket – and best of all, a beautiful little doll dressed in pink.

I squealed with delight – I had never had a real doll before, only black ones our Mother used to make from old stockings. My gran found one of her crocheted shawls and I sat by the roaring fire nursing my lovely doll, while she got on with the cooking.

Into the oven went the pheasant and potatoes for baking while on the hob a monstrous Christmas pudding bubbled and boiled in the great saucepan. Up to her elbows in flour, my gran made pastry for mince pies. Her face was red and shiny where she kept bending and peering into the oven as each batch was drawn out.

For the hundredth time I peeped at my doll, then I let

out a loud scream. 'Whatever is the matter, my little maid?'
my gran said, rushing over to my side.

'Look Granny, look', I cried, my cheeks streaming with
tears. 'My doll's face, it's gone.'

The heat from the fire had melted the pretty wax face;
now all that was left was a shapeless lump. I cried for the rest
of the day. I couldn't even eat. I never did taste the pheasant
we had prepared so excitedly the day before. As my gramp
ate his Christmas pudding he kept finding shiny threepenny
bits. 'Come on my little maid,' he said, 'you might find a
florin in your piece.' But it was no use – nothing comforted
me.

We went to church the next evening, walking down the
beech-lined drive to the village. As we went up the church
path a horrid boy snatched my green tammy off by the bobble, and I punched him so hard he soon dropped it. 'Proper
little spitfire en't you?' he said, but he didn't try it again. My
grandparents were slightly ahead of me, chattering; otherwise they would have chastised me for such unseemly
behaviour so near to the church.

As the lord and lady of the manor took their seats in the
cold, grey, candle-lit church, the women all curtsied. Her
ladyship was dressed in deep purple and sat stiff-backed and
regal. Like a proud foreign bird she looked. The brilliant
feathers round her turban-shaped hat wriggled and fluttered
at the slightest movement. She showed up like a jewel

against a sea of the Sunday-best black of the village folk.

Out in the cold moonlit night once more, goodnights and ''appy New Year if I dun't see 'e agen', was echoed again and again. Then back through the quiet park, save for the hooting owls and scurryings across the leaf-strewn path of things I couldn't see; and I held my gramp's hand tight for fear of being whisked away by witches and hobbly-goblins into the trees.

The next day one of the footmen from the big house knocked at the door of the lodge. He handed a big brown paper parcel to my gran. 'It's for the little girl', he said. We stood there for a moment, speechless.

'Whatever is it, Mr Carter?' my gran asked.

'Well, Mrs Broad, her ladyship heard that your little grandchild had had a most unfortunate accident with her doll. There's a note inside', he said, and was gone.

Still bewildered we went back into the house and I snatched at the wrappings, tearing the paper with excited fingers. 'Careful, child,' my gran warned, 'it might be something breakable.' She read the note pinned on the top of the box, 'For the pretty little girl in the gay green tammy'. Inside was the biggest, most beautiful doll I had ever seen. My gran said that it must have belonged to one of her ladyship's children when they were small. It was dressed in fur-trimmed satin and all the clothes took off, and I undressed that doll a hundred times or more that day I'm sure.

Excitedly I told my gramp about the doll when he came home from work.

He lifted me on his lap and said, 'It's worth all the tea in China to see you laughing again'.

A few days later the baker picked me up. I was to travel back home as I had come, and although I'd got my lovely doll and a parcel of things for the rest of the family I cried when I left my grandparents. 'Come again soon little maid', they said, but I never did.

During the next year my gran died and my gramp went to live with my uncle and aunt at a nearby farm in the village. But I spent some very happy holidays with him there.

We used to sit on the wall near the road and he'd sing to me. His favourite was 'Pretty Polly Perkins from Paddington Green'. I've only got to hear the tune now and I'm back in that quiet Cotswold village sitting on a wall with my gramp.

His hair, once so very black, had now turned to what he called 'pepper and salt' – really sprinkled with grey – and his eyes were the brightest blue, crinkled and laughing. And that's how I last saw him, waving goodbye to me as I rode away in the baker's cart that was to take me to Burford. He had given me two super ripe pears to take home but I remember eating them before we got out of the village.

Sometimes I pass the lodge where my grandparents lived

for so long and where I spent such happy times. The last occasion was on a cold November day. The place was empty and deserted and the curtainless windows had a ghostly air about them. The Cotswold mist was hanging thick in the beech-lined drive, and the last remaining leaves were fluttering quietly to the ground. I had a great urge to stop and peer in at the windows. Never go back they say, so I turned away, leaving undisturbed all the lovely memories of the past.

(from *A Kind of Magic*, Chatto & Windus, 1969)

A winter's day

Father Christmas

FROM GLADYS GARNER

*We lived for many years in a cottage down by the toll bridge in
Eynsham. And every Christmas-time, we used to have several
cousins, aunts and uncles and friends come to visit us.*
*'Course, there wasn't a lot of money about in those days, and how
my mother managed it, I don't know. But she used to get together
little presents and my dad would dress up as Father Christmas and
give everybody a little gift. It was often a bar of soap for the grown-
ups, and we youngsters might have a hankie or a few marbles, or
maybe a sugar mouse, but it was the excitement and happiness that
those little events brought. The one thing that the youngsters liked
was my dad's pianola, which they called his magic piano, and really
believed that he could play the music with no hands.*
*One year some friends of ours came and they had a little boy – I
think he was about seven years old – a most obnoxious child, who
insisted on telling everybody, including the children who still
believed, that it wasn't Father Christmas. 'It is yer mam and dad,
what brings you presents.'*
*Well, this particular year my dad had just finished dishing out the
presents from his sack, when this boy shouted out, 'It 'ent really
Father Christmas, it's Mr Evans. Ha, Ha, I knows it is.' Somehow*

The Toll Gate, Eynsham. Tolls are still paid here even after a couple of centuries

it was all smoothed over, and my dad went off to change into his everyday clothes. But all the evening, the boy kept saying that it was Mr Evans, and the little children started crying. Then my dad had a brilliant idea. He was sat by the fire and the horrible boy was teasing some children over the other side of the room. My dad picked up one of his wellington boots, and catching hold of it by the foot, held it half-way up the chimney.

Still holding on to it, he called to the boy, 'Hey, Graham, look, I've got hold of Father Christmas's boot'.

The boy stared and went dead white, and we never heard another thing from him for the rest of the evening.

My Mum's Baked Rabbit

I can still remember what those baked rabbits tasted like. My mother used to often cook them whole. She could skin a rabbit quicker than you could say 'Jack Robinson'. Mind you, my stepfather used to paunch them (take all the insides out) for her beforehand.

She would lay the whole rabbit, head and all, in a large baking tin, with a basin of stuffing at the ready. Then she would fill the belly part with the stuffing made from breadcrumbs, grated onions, chopped parsley and thyme, and an egg to bind it. Then, with a needle and thread, she would sew the belly up again, so that the stuffing didn't fall out. Around the rabbit she'd place about two pounds of peeled potatoes, cut in halves and a couple of big onions. These were smothered in plenty of dripping. She would take the filled baking tin to the fireplace where a kettle was always boiling on the hob, and carefully drip quite a few drops of water over each potato. Then she'd pop the tin into the fire oven to cook for about two-and-a-half to three hours. Of course the potatoes helped to keep the rabbit moist. With plenty of cabbage, swedes or parsnips cooking on the open fire, we'd all sit down and have a wonderful meal!

Sometimes she would joint the rabbit, smothering it first with lots of sliced onions, followed by plenty of sliced potatoes. A couple of meat cubes crumbled in a cup of water was also added, along with dripping dotted on the potatoes. This tin was covered with another one for about the first hour. Then it was removed to let the potatoes brown and crisp up. Along with plenty of vegetables this made a meal fit for a king!

Carol Singing

Of course carol singing in the days of my youth could be a bit dodgy.

I remember when a couple of the village lads, eager to get a few coppers with their carol singing, called one night on a crusty old bachelor farmer who was known by everyone for his meanness. They were well into 'Away in a Manger' when the bedroom window was flung open and the contents of the chamber pot thrown over them.

'Bugger off, can't you, and let me *lay down my head*. If you'd been working as hard as I have today, you wouldn't want to be woke up with a lot of bloody caterwauling', he shouted, shutting the window back up again with a bang.

When we got older our carol singing was confined to the 'Big House', and a few larger houses where people lived who were much better off than us. With our boots covered with old socks to keep us from slipping on the icy roads, and with candles in jam jars, we'd set off – probably walking miles just for a few coppers. Mind you, at some places we

Ducklington Mill

didn't get any money, but mince pies, hot soup and handfuls of russet apples.

One house we loved to sing at was the mill house attached to the flour mill at the other end of the village, and this was often our last call of the evening. This was where two elderly spinster ladies lived – the Miss Holtons – whose lives were devoted to the church. Our instructions from them were to 'always knock gently on the door'. Then they would come swishing along the cold passages in their long skirts, and invite us in. Our first carol for them (by request) was always 'While Shepherds Watched', and then we'd burst forth with renewed vigour with 'See Amid the Winter's Snow', all the time thinking of the mince pies that they would give us. The Miss Holtons' mince pies were the best we ever tasted, all fatty and crumbly. 'We will tell the rector how beautifully you sang', they would call as we hurried down the dark drive, but our mouths were too full to answer. As soon as we got out on to the road we divided our spoils – 8d each, three apples and bellyful of hot soup, apples and mince pies – not bad for a night's singing; then we made our way home, tired but quite content.

The Christmas Shoot

When my elder brothers, Bern and Bunt, were about thirteen and fourteen, they used to go beating for the local gentry. They were very lucky to go, as many men and boys in the village would have been glad of the chance – but not all were asked. It was a wet and often very muddy job, but the rewards were worthwhile. The Christmas shoot was the best of all, which the beaters looked forward to. For one thing they often received small tips from the visiting gentry, and were always given a brace of rabbits and sometimes the odd pheasant by the farmer, as well as a darn good meal into the bargain. The day's beating usually began at nine o'clock, but they had to get to wherever the shoot started from in good time.

Dressed in all the warm clothes they had got, and with their legs swathed in old army putties and boots, my brothers were ready for the off. The head keeper was very smartly dressed in green tweeds and was very strict telling them that they must keep in line, and no shouting or loud talking so as not to disturb the birds before the 'guns' – the shooting party made up from the landed gentry and gentleman farmers – were in their positions.

VILLAGE CHRISTMASES

Each beater carried a stout stick. This was to whack the tree trunks so as to disturb the pheasants and drive them forward to where the guns were. The event was organised like a battle by the head keeper, for he had to know just where the shooting party was so that the beaters did not go near them otherwise there might have been a serious accident. Miles and miles the men and boys trudged, over muddy fields, through woods and copses, whack-whacking their sticks all the while. At last, an hour's respite at dinner-time. While the gentry went off to the big house to regale themselves in port, wine and game pie – and no doubt many other luxuries – the beaters were also given a slap-up meal. This Christmas shoot was really the only time that they had such a feast. In a big cleared-out barn, where long trestle tables were spread with white cloths, were piles of plates of bread and cheese – my brothers said that was the most tasty cheese that they ever had – then there was hot game soup, jacket potatoes, hard boiled eggs and pickles and chutney of every sort. You can imagine how twenty or more hungry fellows tucked into that food – fell on to it like a swarm of locusts, the head keeper remarked. And soon, my brothers said, every plate and dish was cleared. Along with all that there was a bottle of beer each for the men, and plenty of strong sweet tea for the boys.

Then it was out into the cold wind again, to work until about 3.30 in the afternoon. In the meantime, all the day's game had been picked up and brought to the back of the great house. Pheasants by the dozen there were, and some rabbits and hares. After the gentry had taken what they wanted, the rest were sent off by train to Oxford to one of the big butchers there. If the birds had been shot about a bit, and were not fit to send to the butcher, they were put on one side and afterwards distributed to the beaters, along with two rabbits each – also shot by the guns – and 4s for the day's beating, along with 2s 6d in tips.

My brothers, wet and tired, soon hurried home to present our mother with their day's spoils. She always gave them a shilling back and, of course, they were allowed to keep the tips. But some of the lads' mothers took all the money. My mum reckoned that they had earned a shilling even though, hard up as she always was, she could have done with keeping it all. She said that it was only fair to give them back a bit.

Brummie Edwards from Ducklington was always considered head of the beaters, and was a wily, cunning old fellow. He knew the countryside around like the back of his great gnarled hands. And it was to him that the gentry went to ask him to organise the beaters. One day my brother Bunt saw him hiding a pheasant ina ditch. So Brummie said, cunningly to him, 'That's what you wants to do, my boy. Pick an odd one up now and then and throw him in the ditch quick, then you can slip back at night and pick the bugger up. Them toffs 'ent going to have 'em all.' So that's what Bunt did, thinking all the time that somebody might see him. But all was well, and he went back at night and retrieved it. Our mother scolded him for doing this – grateful as she was for another pheasant. She told him never to do it again.

'You don't want to spoil your good name, just for a pheasant, my lad. Nothing's got by ill-gotten gains,' she told him, and – as far as I know – he never did a dishonest thing again.

But what a feast followed the boys' beating. Four rabbits, two – and once three – pheasants, and for a week or more we lived like fighting cocks. Afterwards my brothers sold the rabbit skins to Benny Clements, the oil man, for sixpence each, and forgetting the mud and the miles of walking, looked forward to another day's beating – and so did we!

And this is how our mother cooked pheasant, when we were very young. She didn't put home-made wine in it, but later on when we were older she did. I still use the same recipe, adding mushrooms, but in her case they were not always available. And, of course, our mother's was cooked in the old fire oven, which I am sure made the dish even more flavoursome.

PHEASANT CASSEROLE

1 pheasant
1 oz flour
Salt and pepper to taste
2 oz dripping

2 oz streaky bacon (home cured in our young days)

2 medium sized onions, sliced

2 oz mushrooms

1 teaspoon each of parsley and thyme

1 pint water, along with 2 meat cubes

1/2 pint red home-made wine (elderberry is best)

METHOD: After plucking the bird and cleaning out its entrails and any food in the crop, wash it well inside. Cut the bird into joints and dip each piece in the seasoned flour. Melt the dripping in the frying pan and fry each joint lightly on both sides for a few minutes. Tip them into the casserole. Chop the bacon small and fry, for a few moments; add the fried onions and tip into the casserole.

Add the mushrooms and herbs and any of the seasoned flour that is left, along with the meat cubes, water and wine and the liver, heart and gizzard. Put a lid on and place in a medium oven (gas mark 4, 375°F/190°C) for three to four hours. If the bird is an old one it will need four hours, but if young and tender two-and-a-half to three hours will be OK.

Of course this wasn't the end of it for my parents. The big tail and wing feathers were always saved to make 'Tater Awks', to scare birds from our garden, and the finer feathers my mother bunched up like a bunch of flowers, secured with some wire, fixed on a stick and – hey presto! a feather duster!

The Magic of Christmas Eve

FROM JOYCE BAUGHAN

Memories from Joyce Baughan

This charming picture of two little girls dressed ready for bed, having hung up their stockings over the fireplace on Christmas Eve, was lent to me by my old friend, Joyce Baughan. She told me this story.

When it hung in Grandma Long's house, we, my sister Mary and I, used to think that it was a picture of us two. In those days children didn't ask questions or go poking around looking at pictures. Then, years afterwards, the picture came into my hands, and written very faintly in one corner are the words 'Copyright 1898. The Allman MFC Co., New York'. I have it hung in my bedroom and still like to think that was how Mary and I probably looked when were around the age of those two little girls.

A Couple of Ducks

Once, a few days before Christmas, our stepfather brought home a couple of dead ducks, lovely fat ducks they were too. 'They'll be a change for Christmas dinner,' he said, 'old Herbert Bayliss sold 'um me.'

'Lovely', our mother cried. 'Who's going to pick 'um, though?'

'I will', I cried. 'Well, only if somebody will scrub the back kitchen and passage for me.'

'Right', our mother said. 'I'll do your scrubbing [this was the job that I had to do every Saturday, and one that I detested] and you pick the ducks.'

The kitchen floor was stone flags – well, some people called them 'slabs', and as I toiled on hands and knees over this weekly job, with only a handful of soda and a big bar of yellow soap, a bucket of luke-warm water and a bit of old rag for a floor-cloth, different members of the family were in and out, and often walking over the freshly scrubbed floor. So, to think that I was going to get out of doing this was wonderful, I thought. Of course, I had to pick the ducks out in what we called the hovel – this was where coal, wood, bikes and the old washing copper was: a dirty, cold old place it was in winter-time.

I found an old raincoat and jammed my beret on my head. Well, at about one o'clock on that Saturday afternoon I started, little realising that ducks have about three or four layers of feathers, and that they need to be picked differently to hens – a job that I was quite good at. So I started grabbing the feathers in handfuls, first from the breast and then the backs. But the birds didn't look much different – they were still covered in feathers, white and thick. Those feathers floated about the old hovel, settling on all the cobwebs, bike saddles and everything! At about half past three, when it was almost dark, I trailed indoors. I was cold and hungry and fed-up, and I started to cry.

'They don't look no different to me', I wailed, holding the offending birds. 'Damn and blast the ruddy ducks, I 'ent going to pick 'um no more. Them as eats 'um must pick the feathers awf 'um. I shan't want any on Christmas Day. I've had enough of ducks to last me a lifetime.'

The family all laughed; I was such a sight. My beret had slipped down almost over my eyes, and I was covered in feathers and down from head to toe, and blue with cold.

'I'll finish them off', my mother cried. 'Perhaps you won't ever grumble about scrubbing the back kitchen after this.'

But many years later, when my Ginger and I kept ducks

Feeding time

and geese, turkeys and hens, I learned that to pick ducks properly you had to push finger and thumb right down to the flesh, pinching out, all at the same time, the four layers of feathers and down that cover them – or those that the fox didn't carry away! But that's another story!

Christmas Day Surprise

FROM SUE CHAPMAN

*One Christmas when we were all young, we went off to bed on
Christmas Eve, and when we got up the next morning our lovely
old farm house was beautifully decorated, complete with a
Christmas tree, even the stair banisters were entwined with ivy, and
we children were speechless – it all looked so lovely. Our parents
must have been up until about three in the morning to have it
looking so beautiful.*
But it was so wonderful, and I have never forgotten it.

Wartime Christmases

Very soon after my husband was called up in the army, I packed up my furniture, stored it in an old garage for 2s a week, and went back home to live with my mother. My son, Peter, was eighteen months old at the time, and I was getting 28s a week from the army to keep us both – so there was nothing else for it, *but* to go back home. After a little while, I got a job as a machinist in the 'Cap Factory', and was paid 32s a week at first, but it did go up a bit afterwards.

So my mother looked after Peter while I cycled up to the other end of Witney to work in what had been the glove factory, but was now making all sorts of 'forces' hats. We worked on a conveyor-belt system: if your machine went wrong, you got all behind, but had to catch up as you were keeping other girls waiting further along the line. We sang and chattered as we worked, but I didn't care for it at all. Stuck in a factory along with about eighty other women every day was not for me – I was used to a bit of fresh air. So when Denis, my youngest half-brother got his call-up papers, I put in for his job – lorry driving for a wholesale

VILLAGE CHRISTMASES

Mollie and Ginger on Ducklington village green, 1940

grocer in the town. 'Course, they welcomed me with open arms: I had already been driving for a few years, and not many females could drive at that time. It was hard work but I enjoyed it, and could lift one hundredweight and two hundredweight of sugar easily, and great wooden crates of cheese and sacks of flour. The job took me all over Oxfordshire, Gloucestershire and into Berkshire, delivering goods to the shops. Some were in the towns but many were right out in the country, and I drove to villages that I had never been to before. When the weather was nice, I used to take my mother and Peter – they loved an outing like that, and it gave them a chance to see different places. All over the Cotswolds we went. Mind you, at first I had a bit of a job to find my way to some of the remote places. You see, by then all the signposts had been taken down (a wartime measure), and apart from a few farm workers, there weren't many folk about to ask the way. But in the end I knew all the countryside around like the back of my hand, and enjoyed the job for nearly six years, until the menfolk began to come back from the forces. Of course, they wanted their jobs back. And then I got another job, doing a lot of farm work – but that's another story.

But that first Christmas Peter and I spent with my mother was quite nice, apart from the fact that my husband, Ginger, was out in France with the army, sleeping in barns and really

Ginger's Christmas card to Mollie and Peter

roughing it. Brothers Bern, Ben and Denis were all in the forces too, although they came home for that first Christmas. Things hadn't got too bad: the shortage of food and such was so gradual that we hardly noticed it that first Christmas. Baubles and tinsel were still available (in fact I have a few of those baubles still to this day), and red candles in little 'pinch on' candlesticks. I bought some blanket pieces from one of the factories and made my Peter a lovely all-in-one bomber suit in camel; I lined the hood with red, and it lasted him for years. In time, of course, it got a bit short in the leg, and then it was passed on to John, his cousin, two years younger than he was – and *he* wore it for ages.

My sister Betty (John's mum) and two-year-old Jennifer and Stan, their daddy, all came that Christmas, and we had a

Ginger in uniform, 1939

99

nice jolly time. We all hoped and prayed that by the next
Christmas the war would be over and everybody back home
for good, but it was not to be: six long years went by before
Ginger was back home with us.

One Christmas at my mother's I remember best of all.
Peter was about three years old and so was Jennifer. We dug
a Christmas tree up from our mother's garden, and after the
children were in bed on Christmas Eve we decorated it.
Both Betty and I had scoured the shops for bits and bobs
and little presents to put on the tree. Of course, it was lit by
the little red candles as there was no electricity in my mother's bungalow until well after the war. When the children
came out on Christmas morning and saw the tree – it was

*Mollie during the war
years*

100

magic! It was a joy to see the delight and wonder on their little faces! They had already had a little stocking each which they had carefully hung up the night before, but this tree was a surprise, so lovely. Mind, we told them that Father Christmas might come later on if they were good children. All day long they behaved perfectly. Betty had made a red hood thing edged with cottonwool; her husband, Stan, borrowed a red dressing gown, and he really looked like Father Christmas. So, when it was dark, he went off and dressed up: we had already put a few little things in a sack.

Now, my mother at the time had one of those wind bell things that you hung near a draught, and it made a tinkling sound. So, I planned to stand up with my head touching the wind bell just as Father Christmas was coming. Later, Betty

Mollie's son, Peter, aged six

said to the children, 'I think Father Christmas is coming'; I stood up, my head hitting the glass wind bell, and there was the faintest wondrous tinkle! 'Hark!' Betty said, 'can you hear his sleighbells?' Their little eyes shot out like chapel hat pegs. There was a knock at the door, and Betty let Stan in: he really looked the part and the children were so excited. My Peter sat on my lap – just a little bit scared. Stan spoke to them in a gruff voice, and then put his hand in the sack to fetch out a little present each.

Then Jennifer, always a bright child, blurted out, 'He's got my daddy's shoes on!' Brown brogues they were – of course things had got a bit short by then, and we couldn't supply him with wellingtons!

I can't remember the reaction to her remark, but I think it all passed off alright. Another treat at Christmas in those days, was a few good thick slices of home-cured ham for supper. You see, we – my mother, stepfather, Peter and I gave up the coupons for our bacon rations and in place of those we were allowed to buy pig food to feed hungry Horace, our name for our pig, and in time we could have our very own and quite plentiful bacon – when the pig was killed in October. Our stepfather used to pickle the hams, buying special pickle mixture from Saltmarsh and Druce's shop in the town. It contained, among other things, brown sugar and juniper berries and spices, all mixed up with old beer. Those hams were absolutely wonderful – I've never

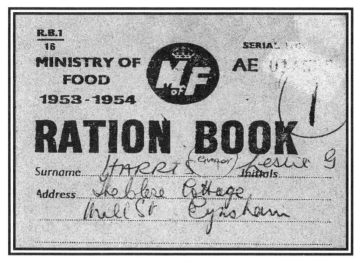

Ration Book, 1953

tasted any as lovely before or since. After our stepfather had rubbed this special pickle into the hams for a few weeks they were then put into an old piece of cheese-cloth and hung up on a nail in the living room to dry out – the best pictures we got in the house, our mother used to say to visitors. And those hams were just fit to eat come Christmas.

The pig-killing days were something special, too. In those days you just asked Mr Humphreys, the local pig-killer, to come up and do the job. Mind you, when the word got round that we were having our pig killed, we always had more visitors on that day than on any other. Folk were so short of food that they almost begged for a bit of pig's fry or half the chitterlings, or back bones that the pig-killer cut out of the animal, to make a boney pie. Of course, it was a busy time for my mother and me. We had to cut up the flear – that's the fatty piece that you make the lard from by melting the small pieces of fat in a saucepan, and then as it melted you had to keep pouring it off. Two or three love-ly basins of pure white lard it made, which we had on our bread for weeks. Our mother always put a sprig of rose-mary in the saucepan when we made the lard – this gave it a wonderful flavour. There were chitterlings to be cleaned and turned and soaked in salt water to get all the muck out of them. But these were lovely when cooked. The sides of the pig were laid in a lead-lined trough that my stepfather borrowed. Salt and saltpetre had to be rubbed into the meat every day to help preserve it. After about three weeks the sides were taken out and also hung up – this time in the back kitchen. When they were nicely dried out, we had bacon for breakfast most days. If the pig was a bit on the fat side, our mother used to make bacon clangers (see p. 105 for recipe). This made a good nour-ishing meal for us. A family in a nearby village were always known as 'Clanger Browns' – 'cos folk reckon they had one of those puddings every day: great big heavy peo-ple they all grew up to be, too.

Village Christmases

Bacon Clangers

(The way my mother made them)

When Christmas was over it was back to bacon clangers, stews and dumplings.

Crust

3/4 lb self raising flour

1/2 lb suet

A good pinch of salt

1/2 teaspoon mixed herbs (parsley, thyme and marjoram)

Water to mix

Filling

About 6 oz bacon (chopped)

1/2 teaspoon mixed herbs (as above)

1 good sized onion

Salt and pepper to taste

METHOD: Mix all the crust ingredients together well to make a stiffish dough. Flour a board, place the dough on it and press with the flat of the hand into an oblong shape. Dot bacon all over the dough, sprinkle on the herbs, cover with finely sliced onion, season with salt and pepper and roll up the pudding into a roly-poly. Pinch the ends up to seal them. Flour a pudding cloth and place the pudding on it, and roll up, sewing it up to seal. (Of course, foil and grease-proof would be used these days.) Put into a saucepan of boiling water and cook for 3 to 3^1/$_2$ hours. Serve with brussels sprouts and carrots. REMEMBER that the water in the saucepan will need topping up several times while the pudding is cooking.

This story of pigs chitterlings is perfectly true, as I knew the person it happened to. There was a man in Witney who kept a lot of pigs, and used to kill one or two most weeks, selling the joints of meat round about. He was a bit on the mean side, and always employed poor boys who had just left school and, most likely, for a while couldn't get any other work. One night, just before it was time to knock off, he said to this lad, 'I'm off, but there's some uncleaned chitlins in that bucket. You can take them home for your mother – not in the bucket, mind.' This lad was so pleased: he knew that his mother would be glad of them. But how was he to get them home? They were so poor that he used to bring his bit of grub wrapped in paper, no money for a sandwich tin or anything like that. Then he thought, 'I'll stuff them in me trouser pocket'. And this is what he did, forgetting there there was a hole in his pocket. He got on his old bike with great difficulty, and started for home. Halfway along the road he caught up with a girl who was walking home from work, and who he was sweet on. So he gets off his bike and walks along with her. Suddenly she looked down and screamed. 'What's that?' she cried, looking at his boots – and promptly fainted. The boy glanced at his feet. The chitterlings had worked down his leg, and there was about three or four inches dangling across his boot. 'Surely,' he told his brother afterwards, ''er never thought my John Thomas was that long!' His brother replied, 'If it was, you'd be on show in a blummin' circus!'

Another lovely thing that our mother made a day or so after the pig had been killed was faggots, made with the pig's liver.

FAGGOTS

1 pig's liver
3 medium sized onions
3 oz chopped suet
4 oz breadcrumbs
1 cup of water
1 tablespoon of mixed herbs (she used sage, parsley and thyme)
Salt and pepper to taste
$^1/_2$ lb streaky bacon

METHOD: Mince the liver and onions and tip into a mixing bowl, add the suet, breadcrumbs, herbs, salt and pepper and mix well. Form the mixture into balls – a bit bigger than an egg. Wrap a piece of bacon around each faggot (or use the cawl instead – which is piece of cobwebby fat from the insides of the pig).

Place all in a baking tin, pour the water around the faggots and cook in a warmish oven for about three-quarters of an hour.

These are lovely eaten hot or cold.

Chrismas Wheelbarrows
and Surprise Parcels

One Christmas, when our son Peter was about fourteen, he decided that he wanted to buy his father a
new wheelbarrow. The one he was using was very old, the
wheels wobbled and it was hard work to push, 'specially
when it was filled with hen or pig manure, after he'd
cleaned them out.

The year before, Peter had bought his Granny Butler a
small wheelbarrow for her Christmas box, and Ginger
remarked at the time that it was just what he could do
with, only a bigger one than Gran's. Peter had bought
hers from Sawyers, one of the local general stores in the
village which at that time sold everything – tools for the
garden, groceries, paints, paper and paraffin, bikes, crockery, shoes and boots: you name it, they sold it. The
wheelbarrow cost him £2 10s. This was in the days when
village folk gladly bought from local shops (there were
three or four of them who sold many useful household
items and groceries), but the coming of the motor car for

Brother Bern, Ginger and son, Peter

the ordinary man killed off these shops, and gradually one by one they closed.

Anyhow, at this particular time, Peter was doing a paper round and had saved up his money for months to be able to buy this wheelbarrow for his dad's Christmas box. He purchased it from Leighs, the ironmonger in the nearby town of Witney, for £3 15s, and it was a good strong heavy one. And he rode home, five miles, to Eynsham with this blummen great wheelbarrow on the front of a trade bike – you know, the sort that shops used for local deliveries, with a basket in the front. Only Peter's didn't have a basket, but just the iron frame where the basket should have sat. And it was on this frame that he perched the wheelbarrow. It must have been a very hard ride for him, up and down those hills. But there was no other way to get it to Eynsham. Leighs certainly wouldn't have made a special delivery for a paltry wheelbarrow, and he didn't know anyone who would have brought it home for him. There weren't many folk about with vehicles in those days.

Well, it was about eight days before Christmas and he didn't want his dad to know what he'd got him for a present, so we decided that we would take it up to the attic. At that time our stairs in the cottage were those old-fashioned twisty narrow ones, and Peter and I struggled to get it up – first to the bedroom. Then we had to get it up the attic ones which were a darn sight more difficult and narrower than

Ginger and Mollie, 1959

the others. After much puffing and blowing, grunting and swearing, we managed to get it up there.

'Well,' I said to him, 'if you think I'm going to struggle to get that damned thing down on Christmas morning, you've got another think coming! Anyway,' I went on, 'I've got a splendid idea. On Christmas morning you say to your dad, "I've got you a good present, come and see, it's in the attic". He'll be that pleased about it; he'll willingly help carry it down.'

You see, at that time we still tried to create special surprises, especially for Peter, for Christmas, and for many years I always made a surprise parcel for him. It was usually wrapped in sheet after sheet of newspaper, or brown paper –

anything I could lay my hands on so that it made a big parcel. And when he'd finally torn all the wrappings off there
was often a big old potato or a lump of coal. But one year I
fooled him! I did four big parcels up – three contained nice
things, and the fourth the usual 'tater. But he had to keep
tearing the paper off all of them, just in case, and strangely
enough his 'surprise' parcel was the last he unwrapped.

But it was all taken in good spirits, and we always had a
good laugh.

Christmas in the Fifties

During the period when we had the smallholding, our cottage – which at that time didn't belong to us – was, according to today's standards, a bit archaic! Our lavatory was a flush type but it was outside in the yard, and the only baths we took were in a six-foot tin bath filled by hand with water from a gas boiler. Then, after your bath, you had to turn round and bale the water out, and tip it down the sink. Oh yes! We had a sink and wooden draining board which Ginger had moved, after about three years, from the living room. During the time it was in the living room I had made a screen from a clothes horse to put around it, lining it with pretty cotton, so at least while were were having our meals or sitting listening to the wireless, we didn't have to gaze at a sink full of washing up.

And what has this to do with Christmas, you ask. Well, with just the sink and the draining board and the cold tap, I had to pull the innards from the Christmas cockerels and dress them ready for the customers to cook them. Sometimes if it was cold I used to pluck the damned things indoors, too, and you can imagine what a glorious mess that made. No central heating, of course, just a small black Victorian fireplace. No running hot water, either, so the work was very hard with none of the present-day amenities. Still, somehow I managed – what you never had you never miss, they say, and to use my brother's expression of me I was as happy as a pig in s. . .! And it was true. I really enjoyed tending the birds, and later pigs, but it was hellishly hard work.

We used to have some lovely Christmas parties during that period, with brothers and sisters, wives and husbands and children all coming to our cottage. I'd spend days cooking and making pies and puddings, and we'd drag in a couple of trestle tables so that we could all sit down to a fabulous meal of turkey and pig meat, with Christmas pudding and custard for afters. Some folks had to sit on planks of wood set upon stools or oil drums. But it didn't matter – there was laughter and lots of chatter, and above all, lots of fun. And the games that we played afterwards were sometimes a bit cruel – well, not really cruel but for some folks not very nice. We were lucky enough to have a housey-housey set (now known as bingo), so after the meal, and with the washing up all done, we'd settle in the sitting room, with a few children and agile visitors sitting on the floor, and have a number of games. Beforehand I had done up lots of little things for prizes – nothing spectacular, as there was not a lot of money about in those days. As well as nice things, I used to do up some not-so-nice things, but at least they would cause a laugh — well, nearly always! Carefully wrapped in lots of paper and making quite a large parcel was the turkey's parson's nose (cooked of course), but I used to stick some feathers into it to make it look more real! I also used to save the feet and legs. If you broke these properly when you were dressing the bird, drawing out all the sinews which then were left on the legs and feet, you could have quite a game with them, catching hold of the sinews and pulling them, which made the feet or claws move, and running after the youngsters with them made the children squeal. Another thing my sister, Betty, and I did was to make some make-believe Turkish Delight. We'd got a nice box that had held some, but we'd already scoffed the contents. So what we did was to peel a large potato and cut it up into small pieces, carefully dipping each piece in icing sugar so that it looked like Turkish Delight, and then wrap the whole thing up nicely so that it looked like a new box of the stuff. 'Course, someone was delighted to win such a prize — and the winner never did let on afterwards when they discovered what the contents really were when they got home. We did this two or three years running, but not to the same folk. And I remember once someone won the box, promptly opened it, took a lump out and ate it without batting an eyelid, and then closed the box up again. Whether or not they were too tiddly on my home-made wine to know the difference, I don't know – but, again, they never let on.

Another daft game we played was with saucers. I went out into the kitchen and with a lighted candle blacked the underneath of all the saucers, but one. The saucers were then given out to everybody with strict instructions not to look at each other, but to stare at me (my saucer didn't have black on it), and to follow my movements. First, I rubbed my fingers underneath the saucer and round the centre, and then stroked my cheeks. Again I rubbed underneath the saucer and stroke my forehead, continuing this until their faces were completely black. Then I said, 'just look at the person on your right and say Hello'. They thought this was part of the game, then there were screams and hoots of laughter at the sight that everybody saw. And the only place they could wash was our little shallow yellow sink in the kitchen. But it was all taken in good spirits.

Afterwards we all sat around the fire and someone would start to tell ghost stories. There was the coach and headless horses and driver that raced at speed over the playing fields at midnight on Christmas Eve – but no one could ever find out why, or where it was supposed to be going. Or the workman who was walking home one dark night when he was joined by another man: they chatted as they walked along; then a woman came out of a cottage with a lighted lantern, and in the yellow light the workman glanced at his companion – whose head was neatly tucked underneath his arm! Then, as suddenly as he'd joined him the man vanished. But the best of all was the story of our very own ghost – and this is how we found out about him.

We had not been living very long in this cottage, when an elderly neighbour said to me, 'Well, Mrs Harris, how do you like living in your cottage?'

I told her that we were delighted, but that we did hear some funny clumping some nights, although, I added, 'my husband says that it's the old timbers'.

'Oh no,' she went on, 'that's the ghost of Old Natty Gibbons.'

'Old Natty Gibbons, who was he?' I asked, flabbergasted.

'Well,' she said, 'he was an old baker who lived there for many years, all on his own except for a pet fox. One night he was carrying a sack of flour across the old loft of yours.' She rambled on. 'They used to keep the flour there, over the kitchen, to keep it dry. You see, bakers used to "start" their overnight dough ready for baking first thing the next morning, 'cos after they'd baked the bread they had to turn round and deliver it. Well, as I said, he was carrying this sack of flour across that loft when he had a heart attack and died – 'cos there was nobody there to help him. Of course, the next morning folks noticed that there was nothing going on at the cottage, and after a while somebody suggested that Natty might be ill, and they broke in and found that poor old Natty was beyond human help. And ever since then at about ten minutes past seven at night he is heard clumping across that old loft – well, so folks who have lived there told me!'

Well, I told my husband and son Peter this story – but they pooh-poohed it as village gossip. But we did hear the clumping sometimes, and still Ginger said it was the timbers contracting or cooling down at night. We didn't tell anybody about this, but Natty got blamed for doors being left open or crockery broken, and the like. Then a few years later, when my son Peter was courting Beryl – the girl he finally married – a strange thing happened. Ginger and I had gone off somewhere for the evening. Peter was in his little workshop that he had bought and erected up the garden and where he used to mend bikes and sell them. Beryl was sitting in our sitting room sewing, with our dog, Sarah, for company. Suddenly, the dog stood up with every hair on her back and tail upright, and her eyes followed something across the room. There was a clumping, and the dog started whinnying. Beryl, scared out of her wits, rushed up the garden to Peter in the shed and shouted, 'Don't you leave me down there on my own again'.

Peter explained about harmless Natty Gibbons; she calmed down, and all was well. After that we talked quite freely to Beryl about Old Natty.

Then, in 1960, our landlady died and we were allowed to buy our cottage. Soon we planned to have a good deal of alterations to bring the property up to more modern standards without spoiling it. We employed the local builders – Pimms – and they were very fair. Knowing how short of cash we were, they suggested that we might do some of the work ourselves, thus saving a good deal of money. One of the jobs that Ginger and I agreed to do was to take the old blue slates and timber from off the lean-to loft, where old Natty Gibbons was supposed to have collapsed. This we did one scorching hot Sunday; we were covered in white dust and absolutely filthy, but of course there was nowhere to have a bath, as by then the builders had removed most of the kitchen: the next day they were to make a flat roof where we had taken the lean-to away. First they removed the old floorboards and in doing this old Natty's ghost must have been laid to rest – as we never heard him again. But, of course, at the time of the Christmas parties he was still with us along with the old loft and the outside lavatory!

So, as I told the story of Natty Gibbons that particular Christmas-time, everybody was dead quiet, as it was coming up to ten minutes past seven. For a few moments we sat in complete silence, save for the crackling of the wood on the fire, and then – there it was – three distinct clumps as if someone had stumbled. At that very moment a spark flew out and landed onto the cat, who leapt up with a terrible squawk. The party folk were really shocked: 'Shouldn't have believed it if I hadn't been here', my brother said. My Ginger saved the day – or night – by asking everyone if they

wanted another toothful of my sloe gin, and Betty and I
went off to make collared head sandwiches and fetch out the
hot mince pies that I had remembered to put on a low light
in the gas stove.

But the relatives who were there on that particular night
never forgot the clumping of Natty Gibbons, and were
really quite sad that he didn't 'appear' any longer after the
renovations.

The collared head I still make when I can buy a pig's head
from the butcher always reminds me of that special
Christmas party that we held: the quietness for a few
moments and the fire crackling, and then the cat squawking
when the spark fell on him – and the stillness of the folk
who were there.

COLLARED HEAD

This is my mother's recipe, but of course there are other
recipes depending on where you come from: different areas
have different versions.

> *1 pig's head and 2 trotters*
> *A few bay leaves*
> *2 good sized onions*
> *1 large carrot*
> *Sprigs of parsley and thyme*

VILLAGE CHRISTMASES

A few sage leaves
Heaped tablespoon of pickled spice
Salt and pepper to taste

METHOD: Soak pig's head and trotters in salt water for a few hours. Drain, cut out the eyes (something else we use for the joke parcel for housey-housey), but leave the tongue in.

Drain well, cover with fresh cold water and place in a large saucepan, adding bay leaves, onions, carrot, a sprig of parsley and thyme and a few sage leaves – and a good heaped tablespoon of pickled spice tied up in a bit of muslin. Salt and pepper to taste.

Cook all until the meat falls off the bones. Remove the muslin bag and pick off the bones carefully, discarding the ears and snout.

On a large dish continue to cut up the meat quite finely; the vegetables will have blended into the liquid. Pour some of the liquid over the meat to make the meat quite sloppy.

Now, grease some basins well and spoon the contents into them, filling them right up. Place a plate on the top of the filled basin and put something heavy on the top to press the contents down. Leave to get cold.

When needed, tip contents out: they will have set into a lovely mould, and slices can easily be cut.

This is delicious with pickle, pickled onions and chutney – in my case all home-made, of course.

A Fox Went out on a Hungry Plight

When we first came to live in this cottage in 1947, our landlady kept quite a lot of chickens on some ground just beyond the cottage, and her entrance was through our backway. This land was almost an acre, all of which belonged to her. When she got older she gave up keeping chickens and rented some of the land to us. This was during the fifties. So we began to keep pigs, chickens, ducks and turkeys. This was my little sideline. I fed the animals, collected and sold the eggs, and dressed the fowl and sold them, but my husband did most of the cleaning out and built several new fowl houses; and I built up quite a little business.

I forgot who, but someone gave me some Muscovy duck eggs, which I placed under a broody hen, and three weeks later seven fluffy ducks were born. As they grew older, those ducks were a bit of a worry. As well as refusing to go in at nights, during the daytime they took to flying round and round the village, and I was always in fear that somebody

Ginger going to collect the eggs

would take a pot-shot at them – for they were some lovely
fat birds and would have made any family a super meal.
Then, later on that year the ducks, along with the turkeys
and cockerels, were duly ordered for Christmas by local
people. I used to do all the killing, plucking and dressing the
birds, and it was a lot of hard work to get them all ready for
the festive season. Then, about ten days before Christmas a
tragedy happened. Those Muscovy ducks (my husband
insisted on calling them Muscovites), would never go in
their house to sleep at nights, but insisted on perching on
the roof of their house, which was only about four feet
high. There had been a sprinkling of snow overnight, and as
I opened the wire door in the area where all the birds were

124

kept I noticed a trail of blood ending at the wall. I looked round: six very muddy headless ducks lay about in the mud and snow – a fox had killed them all, but had just made off with one, hoping to come back for the others in time (this is the usual pattern). Panic! They were all ordered for Christmas. I picked up the dead ducks, laying them on a table in the shed. I didn't know what to do. Later on that morning, I went down to the village to Harris's (no relation), our local butcher, to buy meat for our dinner. It was a nice family business, with the mother of the young men who ran it, helping. I told her my tale of woe – there was no ill-feeling between us because I was selling a few birds. 'I don't know what to do', I said. 'How shall I keep them until Christmas; and they won't have any necks on them – folks likes the neck along with the giblets to make the gravy.' This was in the fifties, and we hadn't got a freezer or a fridge. Mrs Harris was very kind and helpful.

'Go home and pick and truss them, and bring them down here. We'll keep them in the freezer here till Christmas' – they had one of those huge freezers that half-filled one side of the shop. 'And don't you worry about them having no necks. Let's hope the people who've ordered them are a bit tiddly come Christmas morning, then they won't notice 'um missing.'

'Ah,' I said, 'but what about the one the fox took away?'

'Well, you'll just have to explain and sell them one of

your cockerels instead.' I didn't like to tell her that the only spare cockerel was for our own Christmas dinner.

Well, thankfully everything went off alright, nobody mentioned necks, and we had to have a boiled steak and kidney pudding for our Christmas dinner, as the butcher had completely sold out of everything else!

★ ★ ★

During the time that we had a smallholding, I was lucky enough to get hold of some day-old turkey chicks. You see, a young fellow – well, I think he was about seventeen and a friend of my son's – worked on a farm where they reared turkeys. And one night he knocked on the door and said, 'I hope you can keep these in the warm', and out of his coat pockets he fetched three day-old turkey chicks.

Seeing my look of surprise, he said, 'They be weaklings, Mrs Harris, they'd have been chucked out to die anyroad.'

I soon had them under a 'foster-mother' – a small metal surround with a lamp in the centre and with a cover over the top – which kept the birds warm. One died during the night, but the other two looked quite sprightly. The next night the lad brought four more, and this went on until in time I'd got twelve good healthy chicks – having lost a few on the way. When the weather got warmer I put them outside in a little run, where they could pick up bits of grit and stuff.

Then came the day when they were far too big for their present home, so my Ginger set about making them a big wire cage, open on two sides because, we were told, turkeys like fresh air. He also made a floor of wire but as they got bigger and heavier the wire floor sagged where they landed on it after flying off their perches. So this had to be reinforced almost every week. Very magnificent birds they were, too, and would start gobble-gobbling as soon as I walked up the garden path.

Anyhow, the locals were very interested in buying them for Christmas, and all were soon ordered. Then, a couple of weeks before Christmas, one of my customers had to go off and look after a sick father so she cancelled her order for turkey. Just as well, really: the one I'd got earmarked for her was massive. I asked one of the Harris boys (butchers) how I was to kill them: I could wring the necks of the ordinary cockerels and ducks quite well, but these turkeys were something different. Now I realise this was a *very* barbaric way of killing them, but it was how the Harris's killed theirs – and anyhow this was in the fifties – I'm sure things are very different now.

'Well,' Ken said, 'what you wants to do is lay a hoe handle on the ground, catch your bird, place his head under the hoe handle and at the same time place your feet – one at each end – firmly on the hoe. Then hold the turkey by the legs and give him a sharp pull upwards. That'll do it, it breaks their necks.'

So that's how I killed them. Mind you, some of them birds didn't half flap their wings while I was putting their heads under the hoe handle, and the insides of my legs were black and blue with bruises.

But, back to this rather large turkey that Mrs B. had cancelled. During the next few days he just grew and grew, but of course the day eventually came when he had to go under the hoe handle with the rest. So along with the others I picked him. The ordered birds were duly delivered to the customers, and I dressed the 'big one', and put him on the scales – 32 pounds he weighed! Now I knew we couldn't get him in our oven. Thankfully, at that time the local baker used to cook the villagers' Christmas dinners for a small sum. I had to buy a specially big baking tin, and on Christmas morning at eight o'clock my husband and son, Peter, took 'Fred' – for that's what we called him in the end – down to the bakehouse. 'My goe, he's big 'un', the baker said. 'I'll turn him for you about twelve o'clock.'

It was the loveliest Christmas dinner we'd ever had. My Peter's girl, Beryl, had been invited to join us. When I was carving Fred she said, quite innocently, 'Don't put me a leg, will you' – we've never let her forget that statement! Old Fred's legs and thighs were nearly as big as hers!

On Boxing Day we invited quite a number of the family for a turkey supper to help clear it up, and we all had a lovely feed.

VILLAGE CHRISTMASES

A few years afterwards our landlady died, and we had to give up the ground where we kept the livestock. This land was sold for building purposes, but thankfully we were allowed to buy our cottage and the good strip of land that went with it. It was sad to have to sell off the hen houses and wire and posts, and I did miss all the work that keeping the birds had entailed. But strangely enough, another big event in my life was already unfolding – I started writing and later broadcasting my own work, and my first book – an autobiography – called *A Kind of Magic* was published in September 1969, and is still selling. And then, in 1971, I joined the famous *Archers* cast – but that's another story!

★ ★ ★

Once I asked the butcher boys how they always came with a good bowl of giblets to sell around Christmas-time, when most of the people want them from their birds to make gravy with. Many's the time I've bought the odd pound or two from them to make a giblet pie, traditionally eaten on Christmas Eve day.

'Ah,' they told me, 'you wants to save just a bit of this and a little bit of that from each bird – you know, half the liver, an inch off the neck, half the heart and, of course, some of the gizzard. You'd be surprised how it mounts up. Then,' they added, 'there's always one or two customers who don't want the giblets, so that's how we comes with a bowlful to sell. It's what you'd call a trick of the trade.'

So, of course, with this information I did the same, and each year we really looked forward to a giblet pie on Christmas Eve day, made and covered in flaky pastry – absolutely super!

And this is how you make it.

Giblet Pie

Rough Puff Pastry

8 oz plain flour
8 oz lard
1 tablespoon lemon juice
Cold water to mix

Filling

1 lb – 1¹/₂ lb giblets
Water to cover
Pepper and salt to taste
1 teaspoon chopped parsley
1 teaspoon chopped thyme
1 medium size onion, chopped fine

1 meat cube

1 tablespoon flour or cornflour

METHOD: Tip flour into mixing bowl, adding chopped up lard (big as meat cube), also add lemon juice and water to mix, with a knife, into a workable dough. Tip dough on to a floured board and roll out, folding it three times, and roll again. Leave to rest in the cool.

TO MAKE PIE:

Now, tip all the ingredients into a saucepan and gently cook for about one-and-a-half hours, adding a little more water (not too much) as it boils away. Put aside to cool.

Roll out pastry again; leave to cool. Repeat this process once again. Now empty the filling into a pie dish, and put a pie funnel in the centre. Cover with rolled out pastry and brush giblet pie pastry with milk.

Place in a hot oven (gas mark 7, 220 °C) and cook for about thirty minutes or until the pastry is nicely golden – lovely!!!

How Fred was Prepared for Baking

A good tried and tested recipe.

32 lb turkey, picked and dressed

VILLAGE CHRISTMASES

Stuffing

¹/₂ cup chopped parsley

¹/₂ cup chopped thyme

1 large onion chopped finely

Salt and pepper to taste

1 egg

¹/₂ lb sausage meat (plus another ¹/₂ lb for stuffing the neck)

1 lb fine breadcrumbs

A good knob of dripping

I mixed all the ingredients together with the hands, squeezing it and binding it together with the egg and the dripping, to make it a smooth mixture. I placed it inside the turkey's belly where all the insides had been taken out and filled the cavity at the neck end – where the crop was taken out – with the remaining sausage meat. I saved the neck, heart, liver and gizzard to make the gravy with (or giblet pie), cooking them gently in enough water to cover.

When cooked, and then cooled, I mixed a tablespoon of cornflour and a meat cube in and cooked again, stirring all the while until it thickened.

Then I laid the bird in the baking tin, surrounded with plenty of peeled and halved potatoes and two medium-sized onions, with a pound or more of streaky rashers (or bacon bits if your grocer sells them). Then I covered the bird's breast and legs with the bacon – this helps to keep it moist –

and secured the bacon with *wooden* cocktail sticks, and covered the bird and potatoes with plenty of dripping.

I added a half cup of water – and Fred was cooked in a hottish oven for at least six hours – and the baker turned the bird halfway through the cooking.

A Cold Winter

FROM MONT ABBOTT

The winter of 1962–3 was when my old friend Mont
Abbott was what he called 'shupperin' [shepherding] in the
Cotswolds; he had just had a spell in hospital, and this is
what he told me:

The doctor said that I should soon get well because he said I'd got a
stummock as strong as a horse, and I told him, 'No wonder cos I
'as to work like one sometimes'. Last winter [1962–3] was so
awful and that damned near killed I, and 'twas that what finished
my old dog awf. He was going on fer forteen yu see and couldn't
stand all the diggin' out we 'ad tu do. That snowed fer days, the
drifts was up tu me shoulder – thas all we done my old dog and me
was dig the ship out of the snowdrifts – never lost one we didn't. I
fell down twice, prit near done I was, but thur was nobody else to
help, so I 'ad tu pick meself up and get on with it. Thas all we
done they snowy days was feed the ship and dig 'um out the drifts
– ah some of 'um was eight and ten feet deep, I've never sin such
snow all the time I bin shupperin. 'Course, 'tis allus a top coat
colder up yer than tis your side of Woodstock.

134

Christmas with the Grandchildren

I remember one Christmas very vividly. My son, Peter, and his wife, Beryl, had decided that Peter would play Father Christmas to their two sons, Peter Leigh, and Jonathan. At the time young Peter was about six years old and Jonathan four. Beryl had been busy making the Father Christmas outfit, which was very realistic, complete with hood, to which white hair and a beard were attached. Even his wellington boots had a band of white around the tops. We were all invited to their house for the Christmas Day festivities for this particular event, Beryl's mother and father, and Ginger and myself. Of course the children had hung up their stockings the night before, and already had a variety of gifts, but their mother told them that she had sent a letter to Father Christmas to say that if he had time the boys would love to see him. But she warned the boys, of course – 'He'll only come if you are very very good'.

It was a lovely Christmas Day with a good sprinkling of snow. There was not a speck of green to be seen on their

Left to right, back row: Ginger, Mollie, Mr Bruton (Beryl's dad) and Beryl.
Front row: Mrs Bruton (Beryl's mum), young Peter, Peter (Father Christmas)
and Jonathan

lawn, and the trees in the garden had a dusting of snow on them on the side that faced the wind.

So the scene was set for the surprise visit.

About six o'clock my son, Peter, said, 'Well, I'll just go to the garage and get some petrol.' Of course the children were too young to realise that the garage wouldn't be open on Christmas Day.

'Shan't be long', he called, as he left the room. Beryl said, 'I think I'll go and make a fresh pot of tea', and off she went, too. We, the grannies, amused the boys who were anxious to show us what they'd had for Christmas. After a while, Beryl came back with the tea on a tray.

Suddenly there was a knock on the door, and Beryl went to see who the caller was. In a few moments she came back into the room followed by Peter, all dressed up. 'Look!' she cried, 'it's Father Christmas; he's come to see Peter and Jonathan.' My son was very well made up to look older, and he had even got some snow on his wellingtons and a sack on his back. The boys were absolutely flabbergasted and shyly made for the comfort of their grans' laps. Then Peter said, in a different voice, 'Ho, ho, you mustn't be frightened. I've only come to bring you a few presents, as I heard that you have been very good boys.'

Beryl said, 'I think you had better sit down for a rest, Father Christmas; you must have had a busy time for the last few days.'

So Peter sat down, and young Peter went up to him and promptly sat on his lap, with Jonathan standing near. They just gazed at him, absolutely fascinated. Well, he chatted to them and found a few little presents in his sack for them. After a while, he said that he would have to be going as he'd got a lot of children to call on, and then he added, 'My reindeers who are out on your lawn might be getting a bit restless and eager to go flying off over the rooftops, because we've got a long way to go tonight.'

Very reluctantly the boys said 'goodbye' to him, and off he went with a wave of his hand.

The boys chattered like billyo about the visit, and the toys
that Father Christmas had given them. It was such a wonderful thing for them. After a while my son came back into
the room – of course he had shed all his make-up and was
his old self again. The boys fell on him with excitement.

'Daddy, Daddy, you just missed HIM.'

'Who have I missed?' he asked them.

'Father Christmas!' they shouted. 'He was here, and he
was ever so big and fat and tall – taller than you – and he
gave us some toys, but he had to go 'cos he's got a lot of
other children to call on.'

Then my son said, 'How did he get here? He couldn't
have come down the chimney because we've got a fire.'

'No', they said. 'His sleigh and reindeer were waiting for
him out on the lawn.'

'Let's go and have a look to see if we can see where they
landed', my son said. And we all trooped out into the cold,
snowy, frosty moonlight night, and a snowy owl floated by
on the look-out for his supper. And we all pretended to
have a look around for a few minutes – and then there was a
yelp from Peter. For there on the lawn were definite marks
in the snow as if a sleigh had landed there, and just in front
of it were several marks of the reindeers' hooves. The boys
were speechless, and we grown-ups all oh'd and ah'd. 'See,
Daddy, we told you he'd been.'

We all went back indoors, the boys chattering incessantly

about the sleigh marks and the visit of Father Christmas. Soon it was time for the boys to go to bed, although Beryl said afterwards that they were much too excited to go to sleep and chattered for ages to each other.

Afterwards I asked my son how he had made the sleigh marks in the snow, because they were quite realistic. 'That was easy,' he said, 'I made them with the side of the broom head, and the reindeer footmarks I just did by holding my fingers closely together, and digging the tops of this bunch of fingertips into the snow at appropriate spaces.' Pure Magic!

My grandsons are now aged twenty-seven and twenty-five, and still remember the event vividly.

★ ★ ★

But not all the Christmases were fun and games and stocking filling, parsons' noses and ghosts. There were the Christmases all through the seventies and eighties when I used to organise bazaars for the Cancer Research Campaign, and I often got celebrities to come and perform the opening ceremony. Those bazaars, along with jumble sales held during the year, often brought in £1,000 annually for the charity. Mind you, it was a lot of hard work.

I remember one year, very near to Christmas, the amount had only got to £906 and we didn't think we were going to

*The carol singers from St Leonard's Church group, Eynsham, in Mollie's cottage
for a warm-up and a drink*

reach our target. I rummaged around in our house, and took
things down to the antique shop and raised a few more
pounds. Then the local church choir went round carol
singing – as they did most years – with a little old organ on
the back of a farm trailer, and raised a fair bit of cash. They
used to end up in our cottage frozen, thirsty and hungry. So
it was out with the hot toddy, made from my home-made

wines, and mince pies and sausage rolls – which again was extra work for me. But still, after all that, were were short by £29. Then along came a surprise letter. It was from members of the Oxford Welsh Male Voice Choir, who had heard of our dilemma, with a cheque to make our total up to £1,000.

My mum would have said of that surprise gift, 'If the Lord don't come, he sends.' And we were all very grateful and happy to think the target had once more been reached.

But those sales took a lot of organising, collecting, cajoling, sewing, making of Christmas gifts and decorations, and begging for raffle prizes. Mind you, I had three or four good ladies who made and knitted things for the sale. But 95 per cent of the things sold at those bazaars were piled in our cottage – bedrooms, sitting room, kitchen and garage – heaped high with boxes and parcels, and during the last week before the sale, folk kindly brought things for it. By the actual day there was no space at all in the cottage. Then came the transporting of it all to the hall, which meant several journeys loading and unloading, pricing, organising helpers, and so on. Then there was all the entertaining of the celebrity who was going to open the bazaar.

After the event was over, all the goods not sold had to be packed up and taken back to our cottage, and stored in the spare bedroom until the next Christmas. Then the raffle prizes had to be delivered, notices of amounts raised sent to local papers and radio station, and the cash counted up and sent off to the Cancer Research Campaign.

No wonder that I was completely exhausted come Christmas, and often ended up with flu, a severe cold or terrific nose bleed – mind you, we always had a lovely Christmas dinner with all the trimmings, with the cottage decorated, complete with tree. We even went off on holiday a couple of times – but there's nothing like Christmases in your own home.

Then in Christmas 1981 I decided to stop raising money for Cancer Research, and have a rest. But the next summer, when my garden was full of sweet-peas and other summer flowers, tumbling and sweet smelling all over the place, I though – why don't I sell some for a charity? So, that was it, I started all over again – but this time it was for a local hospice for cancer patients, attached to the Churchill Hospital – Sir Michael Sobell House – and again raised a lot of money annually for them. My last Christmas sale in 1991 raised over £400, and that was really to be the last – doctor's orders! He said, 'You've raised money for charities for long enough; let somebody else have a go.' He was right. I'd been having jumble sales and the like since 1951.

I remember years ago when my friend, Mrs Webb, and I roamed the village with a wheelbarrow collecting jumble, to help to buy some small wrought-iron gates for the old big school here in the village. Those gates are still there: they

Mollie with helpers at the last Christmas sale for Cancer Research, 1981

were made by Burdens, the village blacksmith, to commem-
orate the Festival of Britain and cost £58. I think we raised
just over £30 towards them, and I expect the rest was made
up by children and their parents' donations.

Then the death of my sister Betty from cancer, over thirty
years ago, started me raising thousands of pounds over the
years for Cancer Research.

TV in Mollie's Cottage

One year just before Christmas a camera crew came from Midlands ATV, based at Birmingham, with Geoff Mead in charge of the proceedings, came down and filmed my cottage which was beautifully decorated for Christmas. I invited some of my village friends which included Keith Green and Robin Saunders and who sang the Eynsham Poaching song and played their accordians. Keith is the young man who got the Eynsham Morris team going again, and now they dance all over the countryside and are often asked to visit other countries. I had made dozens of mince pies and a huge bowl of punch from my home-made wines. We sang and joked and told tales of Christmases long gone. The log fire blazed and all our faces, including those of the camera crew, were red with the warmth from the fire and the strong punch, and a lovely time was had by all.

VILLAGE CHRISTMASES

THE EYNSHAM POACHING SONG

Three Eynsham chaps went out one day
To Lord Abingdon's manor they made their way,
They took their dogs to catch some game
And soon to Wytham Woods they came.

CHORUS Laddyo laddyo foldiroll laddyo.

They hadn't been long a-beating there
When one of the dogs put up a hare,
Up she jumped and away she sprang
At the very same time a pheasant ran.

CHORUS Laddyo laddyo foldiroll laddyo

They hadn't beat the Woods all through
When Barrett the keeper came in view.
When they saw the old bugger look
They made their way to Cassington Brook.

CHORUS Laddyo laddyo foliroll laddyo.

When we gets there it's full to the brim.
Well you'd have laughed to see us swim –

VILLAGE CHRISTMASES

Ten feet of water if not more.
When we gets out our dogs came o'er.

CHORUS Ladyo laddyo foldiroll laddyo.

Over hedges and ditches, gates and rails,
The dogs followed after behind our heels –
If he'd have catched us, say what you will,
He'd have sent us all to Abingdon Jail.

CHORUS Laddyo laddyo foldiroll laddyo.

*Mollie as Dame in the
WI Christmas
pantomime*

Home-made Christmas fare, along with hyacinth bulbs that will bloom in a few days time

Even the paintings on the candlestick help to remind us of Christmas time and sliding and skating on frozen ponds; the crocheted pelmet filled with glass marbles from lemonade bottles remind us of another day long ago

Just a few of the many Christmas cards Mollie receives, along with colourful
'Chinese lanterns' grown in her garden which help to brighten up a dark corner

Father Christmas, a wine basket for a sleigh filled with bits from crackers, all set on an old mirror – sprinkled with foil round the edges for frost – I call this my frozen pond. The children love it

Mollie's beautifully decorated cottage lends itself to holly garlands, shiny brass and trailing ivy. And sitting by the log fire is just the place for a tipple and a mince pie

*A little of what you fancy does you good – well somebody's got to try it out for
taste and strength – and it helps to bring out the spirit of Christmas*

Ducklington church and pond. The church remains the same, stone built and strong, but the pond is much smaller these days and surrounded by shrubs and flowers. In Mollie's young days, Druce's cows came down to stand hock high and drink, and when it froze in wintertime children would slide on it for hours.

Candlelight and firelight create a warming picture in Mollie's cottage

The Bell Ringers

These memories of Ducklington came from John
Sparrowhawk whose gran – Mrs Glenister – and later
his parents, Mr and Mrs Sparrowhawk, kept the Bell Inn
there for many years:

The Bell Inn ran a slate club, with Fred Godfrey secretary
and my gran treasurer. On club nights, Fred Godfrey
would set up office in the smoke room and members
would come along to pay their subscriptions. Then, just
before Christmas time, the funds that were left after pay-
ing out sick pay to the qualifying members, would be
shared out and distributed in time for Christmas. There
was also an annual smoking concert held at Christmas-
time in the upstairs section of the brew house of The Bell
(used by the Home Guard as HQ during the war), where
an evening of food and drink was supplemented by
entertainment provided by the members themselves.
Mountains of sandwiches (no sliced bread!) and other
goodies were prepared during the afternoon, and beer
barrels set up ready for the evening. As a child I was

allowed to attend some of these festivities, and well remember one of the favourite songs performed by Mr Freddie ('Oxford') Ayries: he was carter for Farmer Boggis. The song was about the old church bells, and was always sung with gusto. I also remember my own mother singing 'The Mountains of Mourne', and others.

Some of my memories of Christmas are very poor; perhaps it is because we had to take it in turn to help serve in the bar on Christmas Day. But the annual treat for dinner on that day was a chicken which was cooked in a 'tin oven' on a three-burner paraffin oil stove in the brew house. I also remember delicious ham – which again was cooked on the oil stove – for our Christmas and Boxing Day tea. It was the only day of the year when customers went home promptly for their meal – very different from the usual Sunday lunchtime when it was a job to get them gone.

For several years I sang in the choir at church, and at Christmas-time we received sixpence from the rector, the Revd Tristram, and a mince pie from the organist and choirmaster, Mr Harry Steptoe – whose son, Patrick, later became famous for medical reasons. Mr Steptoe used to cycle from West End, Witney, down to Ducklington Church once a week for choir practice, and twice every Sunday to play the organ. But once a month a service was held in the little church at nearby Cokethorpe.

We also received a hot-cross bun at Easter – this, along with the Christmas gift, was our full reward for singing in the choir every week of the year.

You could say I made history at Ducklington in 1938 because at Christmas-time I broke my leg in the vestry of our church – St Bartholomew's. This had an effect on the village, as up to that time no one had had to pay for an ambulance. But my parents received quite a large bill for this – to the horror of the villagers – and as a result an

Church, school and pond at Ducklington

149

insurance scheme was started in which the villagers paid a few pence a week in case the need arose in the future.

I was at the Pebble Mill studios just after I had received the letter from John Sparrowhawk, and mentioned the fact to my colleague, Bob Arnold, about Freddie ('Oxford') Ayries, singing the song about the church bells – knowing that Bob has a great collection of English folk-songs and, many years ago, made a record of some of the songs, which included the church bells one. Bob said that in his younger days he went to Ducklington where he first met 'Oxford' Ayries (so called, some say, because Oxford was the furthest he had ever travelled). But how did he know the tune, I asked him. 'Ah', he replied. 'In those days I used to go as a guest to many a British Legion meeting to sing. I got no pay for this, as I was – and still am – a member of The – now the *Royal* – British Legion. Well, "Oxford" was always at those meetings at Ducklington and he always sang the church bells song. So that's how I picked up the tune, listening to him. He also used to sing a rather naughty song about a German clockmaker. I don't remember all the words, but the last line was, "I will never wind up the clock of another man's wife." And although – as I said – I collected the tune from Ducklington, I could never remember the complete song. But years later, someone gave me a bundle of newspaper cuttings from *The Wilts and Glos. Standard*, printed in 1914 or '15, and in it were the complete words. These, along with many others, were from *Folk Songs from The Upper Thames*, collected by Alfred Williams around the early years of the Great War, and it is said that his version of "The Bell Ringers" was given to him by the Trinder family from the Oxfordshire village of Shilton, who folk reckoned were related to the late Tommy Trinder.'

Bob kindly lent me a copy of the song, which must be about Christmas-time as it takes place when the ringers were *supposed* to ring the midnight peal.

THE BELL RINGERS

Ah those old church bells, those merry bells,
Although there were but three;
A jolly set of ringers they, as ringers ought to be.
It happened once upon a time, how long I can't reveal,
Those old bell ringers sallied forth, to ring their midnight
    peal.
They spent their evening hours before, in soaking well their
    clay
And as they sallied forth that night, could scarcely find their
    way.
To hear them talk, and see them walk, along the road 'twas
    rich;
The truth to tell, one old boy fell and tumbled in the ditch.

VILLAGE CHRISTMASES

CHORUS

Oh it really is a funny thing, the tales that I've been told
And plainly shows what ringing was in the merry days of
   old.

The other two they got him out, and to the church   repaired;
Unlocked the door, and on their knees went scrambling up
   the stairs,
Took off their coats, and seized the ropes but 'twasn't long
   afore
The big bell ringer, missed his pull and finished on the
   floor.
Then getting up, he seized the rope, but found 'twas all in
   vain
For every time he tried to chime he would fall down again.
The other two, their eyes were shut, but still they kept on
   ringing
Till he cried 'stop! let's have a drop, and finish up with
   singing'.

CHORUS

The bells went off with *three, two, one,* and then with *one,
three, two,*
For ring 'em right, that very night, was more than they
   could do.

VILLAGE CHRISTMASES

They blowed, they lugged, they pulled, they tugged, but
   couldn't ring at all,
Until each man had made a stand with his back against the
   wall,
The bells they stopped and down they sat, upon the belfry
   floor.
They drank till all their beer had gone, of that you may be
   sure.
Then groping back their way downstairs, as homeward they
   did reel,
Each man declared had never heard a better midnight peal.

CHORUS

[Words noted by Alfred Williams in '1910's'. This variant
learned by Bob Arnold from the singing of Fred Ayries of
Ducklington in the thirties.]

Christmas Celebrations at Ducklington, 1987

In 1987 there was a delightful Christmas event for the people of Ducklington – the village of my extreme youth.

The BBC producer of *The Countryside in the Seasons* (Radio 4), Caroline Elliott, suggested that we should do a programme on how Christmas was spent in a village at the present time, and I – being presenter of the programme – suggested Ducklington. It is only five miles from my present home, and a place very dear to my heart. I visit often and chat to the locals, visit the flower shows, and talk to the schoolchildren on life as it was when I was at school there many moons ago. And I knew that the villagers usually did something rather special for Christmas.

Well, I set the wheels in motion by arranging a meeting at my old school (still used, along with a modern one), of some of the people who were very much involved with the village community one way or another, and one that the producer, Caroline Elliott, and myself would attend to talk

Ducklington village school that Mollie attended and left at fourteen

things over about what and how each person could con-
tribute to the programme. This was all sorted out and we
made a date for the recording. The rector's wife, Gwyneth
Drummond, who produced the Christmas story of the baby
born in a stable, said that she hoped that the donkey would
not behave as it did the year before, when with Mary on its
back hanging on for grim death, he made off to chase a
pony halfway across the village. The pony was supposed to
carry one of the wise men, but apparently donkeys don't
like ponies!

Just before Christmas, the great day dawned cold and
frosty, and we started to record the programme which

actually took us a couple of days to do. Martin Muncaster and I did the interviewing between us. Firstly he talked about – and afterwards we both attended – the Children's Christmas Festival, held in the new school and organised by the teachers. It was a lovely occasion with many of the village people there, including, of course, all the mums and dads, grans and gramps, uncles and aunts of the youngsters who attended the school, and who made up most of the Festival – which was a mixture of ancient and modern themes on Christmas – mummers, handbell ringers, little plays and carols – and the children were marvellous.

A turkey farmer was interviewed, so too was a local artist and painter of wildlife, a retired schoolmistress, the history group, the innkeeper and a folk-singing group, and Martin attended the Ducklington Women's Institute Christmas party.

But the highlight was the old Christmas story – again mostly played by the schoolchildren. Some of it was performed in the village church of St Bartholomew, some on the green, and it ended up outside the Bell Inn. As we entered the lovely old church on a cold frosty day, a sweet young voice was singing 'Away in a Manger'. Then there were short readings telling the beginning of the Christmas story, and carols. A loud braying of the donkey could be heard above the singing. Then we all moved outside into the brisk, frosty air where Mary was sitting on the noisy donkey. Then Joseph led her carefully down the church path.

One of the items Mollie presented in The Countryside at Christmas *from Ducklington, 1987*

After a little while we all walked towards the village green, where the shepherds were minding their (real, live) sheep. One of the shepherds noticed a very bright star, and they agreed to follow it.

Meanwhile Mary and Joseph had reached the door of the Bell Inn. Joseph knocked and when the innkeeper answered it, Joseph asked for shelter for his pregnant wife. But the innkeeper said that there was no room in the inn, but there

The Bell Inn where Joseph and Mary came but there was 'no room at the Inn'

was a barn at the back they were welcome to use. So Mary and Joseph went off very dejectedly towards the barn.

Then in a little while the shepherds, followed by the wise men, slowly walked up the lane towards the barn, carrying their gifts for the Baby Jesus. We – the crowd – then made our way up the lane, towards the inn, and the sweet young voices of the schoolchildren sang 'Away in a Manger' – and there wasn't a dry eye among us!

This delightful programme was broadcast on Christmas Day, 1987. For the people of Ducklington it complimented the way in which the village still holds together the old and the young, the new residents and the folk who were born there, working and living in a modern rural atmosphere, growing up and growing old in the lovely village of Ducklington.

The Nativity Play

FROM ARTIST GARY WOODLEY

My very first memories of Christmas were when I was about three years old, and I had a beautiful teddy bear which I kept for years. 'Course at the time I thought that jolly old Father Christmas had brought it, but years later I learned that my dad – who had been invalided out of the navy after his war time service – had made him for me. The toy-making was part of the therapy which he, and many other men, were taught to do. And that ted was so beautiful that all the relatives and friends wanted him to make some for their children – and no doubt my dad was quite glad for the extra orders that it brought.

The next most vivid memory was when I was about nine years old, or ten. We children from Ducklington School were for weeks practising for a nativity play. We were all very excited about this. To think that we were going to play our parts in the village church with all our mums and dads watching. But on the night of the performance, quite a number of the cast suddenly became sick. One minute they were alright, and the next they were quite ill. Halfway through Joseph saying to Mary, 'You'll have to have the baby . . .' he got no further, but made a bee-line off the stage to be sick

Gary Woodley with Teddy that his father made

somewhere. Mary carried on for a few moments, but she, too, had to make a dash. It was absolute bedlam. But nobody stopped – they just went on playing their parts. The first shepherd had just got one foot on the stage when he had to turn round to be sick somewhere.

The second shepherd got on to the stage, but promptly fell backwards off it. Now it was my turn, I was one of the three kings. 'Go on, Gary', I heard one of the teachers at the back whisper. I started walking towards the stable, clutching my frankincense in my hands. Suddenly one of the other teachers rushed forward, waving her arms

160

as if to stop the proceedings, and said, 'It's all over, Gary, we're not
doing any more.' At that moment the second king bumped into me,
falling and stumbling in the aisle.
'Coo,' I thought, 'all that rehearsing and dressing up for nothing!'
But strangely enough I didn't get the sickness bug; neither did
Denise, the girl who played the Angel Gabriel, who just stood at
the back of the stage on a stool. But of course she had no words to
say, and all the while was trying to look solemn and angelic.
Afterwards she said to me, 'I've never seen anything like it. The
children came and went at such a speed. At one time the only thing
on the stage was a doll wrapped in an old shawl – who was
supposed to be Baby Jesus.'

Christmas Decorations

During the seventies I did a good bit of TV work, interviewing country people and visiting places – Mr Garne from Aldworth and his famous flock of Cotswold sheep, the Rollright Stones, the history of Woodstock glove-making, and many others. I also did a lot of Christmas decoration demonstrations at Women's Institutes and other organisations. I was then asked to do some on BBC Midlands Television.

At that time, even if there was such a thing as an oasis to fix flowers in, I didn't know about it. But I often made use of a large potato wrapped in foil with holes jabbed in with a meat skewer, before arranging a Christmas decoration, along with holly and ivy and larch branches. I made large arrangements and small ones for a table or sideboard. Sometimes I'd whiten cone-covered larch branches with ceiling whitening and hang coloured baubles and things on them, and sometimes I'd spray the arrangement with gold and silver spray. Another thing I used to make was a kissing bough from metal coat hangers, covered, of course, with foil and looped with red ribbons and hung with little red apples and baubles, and with red candles clipped on – again using evergreens.

Well, I made arrangements to go up and do some Christmas decorations on TV about a week before Christmas. While I was busy collecting greenery from the hedgerows an old lady came up to me and asked me what I was collecting the stuff for. I told her.

'Well,' she said, 'don't forget if you used holly then you must use ivy as well.'

'Why?' I asked.

'Because holly be a man and ivy a clinging woman, and it's bad luck if you don't use them together.'

All that morning I was busy making small arrangements that I could carry in my large basket, along with sprays of ever-greens, holly, ivy, candles and baubles, so that I could actually demonstrate how to do a large Christmas arrangement on TV. I was almost ready to leave – first to catch a bus to Oxford, then by train to Birmingham – when I suddenly thought of another small arrangement I could do using an old brass candlestick, and very quickly assembled it (in the kitchen – which was wrong anyhow), sprayed it with gold spray, popped it into my basket, and then made a dash for the bus. I was soon on the train and making for Birmingham.

I was used to the studio, and quickly assembled my decorations with a word to the studio manager and director about what I was going to say and do.

Well, all went very well – it was live on the evening programme – and everyone was pleased with what I'd done.

Instead of staying for a meal afterwards, I quickly made
for the railway station and was soon on my way home. I had
told Ginger what train I'd be catching, so that he could
meet me in Oxford. I had left instructions on what he could
cook for his tea – eggs and chips was about his limit – and
he was to be sure to watch the programme.

Bless him! he was there waiting for me and grinning from
ear to ear, and we were soon on our way back to Eynsham.
He was extremely chatty and praised my performance on
the TV. Oh yes, he was proud of what I did – but this
enthusiasm was rather unusual for him. We were nearly
home when he said, solemnly, 'Oh, by the way, the kitchen
looks a bit different to what it did this morning'.

'What do you mean?' I cried, sensing something was
wrong.

'Well,' he said, 'what happened was I was very busy cooking my eggs and chips, and was just dishing it up when I
thought, my goodness, I forgot to open the kitchen window
while I was cooking, and the place stunk to high heaven of
fatty fried food. And knowing what you think of cooking
smells, I grabbed what I thought was the air freshener and
really went to town and sprayed the kitchen up and down
and round and round, ceiling and all. But – it didn't smell
like air freshener. Then I realised I'd only picked up some of

your gold spray that you'd left on the draining board. So instead of those kingfishers [we had recently papered the kitchen with rather expensive washable paper], and the bullrushes and reeds and water, looking like a lovely country scene, the complete kitchen – ceiling, cooker, everything, is now festooned all over with gold circlets, and looks like a gin parlour.'

What could I say? It was my fault for leaving the spray there. Well, we didn't repaper for quite a while, and my revamped kitchen was the talking point for months. We were having quite a big Christmas party a few days later, so everybody had to go and have a look and a laugh – and it was the highlight of the evening.

MOLLIE'S MINCEMEAT, AND COOKING A LARGE TURKEY AT HOME IN THE NINETIES

These two recipes are tried and tested, and delicious! First, the mincemeat:

$1^1/2$ lb peeled apple, chopped finely (or put through a coarse mincer)
$^1/2$ lb currants
$^1/2$ lb sultanas
$^1/2$ lb mixed peel

$^1/_2$ *lb stoned raisins*

$^1/_4$ *lb ground almonds*

$^1/_4$ *lb whole almonds (peeled and chopped very finely)*

Rind and juice of 1 orange

Rind and juice of 1 lemon

2 lb soft brown sugar

$^1/_2$ *lb suet*

$^1/_2$ *teaspoon mixed pudding spice*

$^1/_2$ *teaspoon nutmeg*

$^1/_4$ *pint of old ale, or home-made cherry brandy, or sloe wine*

METHOD: Mix ingredients together well.

This is how a friend of mine cooks her rather large turkey. I think, perhaps, the method comes from the fact that busy farmers' wives had to think of some way of getting their bird really cooked for Christmas Day. Anyhow, this is how my friend manages to get her turkey cooked.

After coming home from midnight mass, she places the turkey, all stuffed and ready, in a *very slow oven*, and there it stays until she gets up on Christmas morning. Then the heat in the oven is turned up, so that by 11 o'clock the bird is thoroughly cooked and brown. She takes it out of the tin, wraps it up well with tin foil, then binds the whole thing up with a couple of big thick bath towels (kept especially). This keeps the bird *hot* and stops the steam from coming out which helps to keep the turkey moist, leaving the oven free for a tin of baked potatoes and parsnips.

Giblet gravy already made can also be kept warm at the bottom of the oven. The turkey is still piping hot and carves much better than it would if it had been taken straight out of the oven.

Magical Moments of Christmas-time

For the next twenty years the Christmases flew by. The grandsons were growing up – from Dinkie toys to roller skates, from bikes to girls. And the older they got the Christmases seemed to be less exciting. True, there was always the element of surprise when the presents were opened, and every year I go to town with decorating the cottage: thankfully it is the sort of place – with its old beams, open fireplace with inglenook seats – which lends itself to lots of holly and ivy, kissing boughs, with a garland of evergreens dotted with red bows across the great beam over the fireplace, and always, of course, a Christmas tree, and I still make Christmas puddings, cake and mincemeat.

But Christmas really is for those little children who still believe in the magic of Father Christmas, and everything connected with him. Some children leave a mince pie and a drink of home-made wine, while others leave a mince pie and a glass of port – and it is always gone by the morning, of course!

VILLAGE CHRISTMASES

Up until ten or eleven years ago the family came to us on Christmas Day. For several years it was always turkey with all the trimmings. Then, for a number of years we had roast pheasant – but not like the toffs have it with no stuffing and brought to the table with its original tail feathers stuck up its backside. No, ours were stuffed with stuffing made from parsley, thyme, onion, sausage meat and breadcrumbs, all bound together with an egg and a knob of dripping. Those pheasants, two always, would be covered with streaky bacon held in place with *wooden* cocktail sticks. I did that because, if you are not careful cooking them, pheasant can be a bit on the dry side. And, of course, they were basted a few times during the cooking.

But now, since Ginger died in 1982, I go to my son, Peter's, and his wife, Beryl – along with the boys and their families – for Christmas Day, when we have either turkey or a monstrous cockerel for dinner. But they all come to me on Boxing Day. Now it's not roast pheasant, but pheasant casserole – there's no fear of the meat being dry and, cooked in wine, this makes a most delicious meal.

Another thing I've done for many years is to make most of my own Christmas cards using pressed flowers. Some I pick wild like Kek (Cow-parsley, or Ladies' Lace to the uninitiated) and buttercups – both these press well but I take particular care not to pick anything rare. Small leaves and grasses are very useful, too. Other blossoms I pick from the

Mollie's home-made Christmas card

garden – and how do I press them? Well, someone once gave me a small press which is very useful, but doesn't hold many. For the bulk of the flowers I use an old hardback atlas, long out of date. I lay the blossoms either on lavatory paper or paper hankies – both can be used for their original purpose once you have made use of the flowers. Then the atlas is slipped under the big cushion in my armchair. Some visitors make a bee-line for it because it looks comfortable and inviting: if they look uncomfortable, I tell them what they are doing is helping to press my flowers!

The placing of the book under the cushion always reminds me of how my mother got her sheets and pillow-slips smooth. She never ironed them, but just folded them

VILLAGE CHRISTMASES

*Mollie with her first great-grandchild,
Naomi, Christmas 1991*

up and smoothed them lightly, then placed them under the
chair cushions in the cottage where we lived in Ducklington
– where they were, she used to announce, 'well and truly
ass-ironed'.

And although perhaps the last few Christmases haven't
been quite so exciting, at least for me, things are about to
change for the better. In July 1991 my great-granddaughter
Naomi was born. Of course last Christmas, at five months
old, she didn't really know a lot about it, but for the next
few years the magic of it is about to start all over again.

The wonder of a shining Christmas tree hung with
baubles and draped with tinsel and little tiny gifts for little
tiny hands – the explanation of Father Christmas coming,

and the wonderment on her face at the joy of it all, and the real reason for the celebrations. The excitement of hanging up her stocking, and the magic of finding that filled stocking with whoops of joy at its contents. Yes, it's about to start all over again, the magic of Christmas through a tiny child's eyes.

God Bless Naomi, and may she have many magical Christmases.

Acknowledgements

To all my friends and relations, I offer my most grateful thanks for all the snippets about their Christmases, also those who lent me old photos, which help to portray the Christmases of yester-year: Bob Arnold, Joyce Baughan, Michael Broad, Mrs Lily Bridgewater, Sue Chapman, Caroline Elliott, Gladys Garner, my son Peter and his family, the Harris brothers (butchers), Mr and Mrs John Haslam, Miss E. Holton, John Kempson, Mrs S. Longhurst, Mrs Agnes Neiland, Mrs S. Oakley, Helen Peacocke, Mrs A. Seacole, John Sparrowhawk, Ken Stout, Edna Smith, and Gary Woodley, along with others I've not named. Thanks also to Chatto & Windus/OUP for allowing me to use excerpts from *A Kind of Magic*, and Westgate Library, Woodstock Museum and the Oxford Mail for the use of their photos.